THE GLAMORGAN POTTERY, SWANSEA
1814–38

The GLAMORGAN POTTERY
SWANSEA
1814~38

HELEN L. HALLESY

GOMER

This book is dedicated to the memory
of my mother, Rosina, who first opened
my eyes to the treasures of the past.

First Impression—November 1995

ISBN 1 85902 288 X

© Helen Hallesy

All rights reserved. No part of this book may be reproduced,
stored in a retrieval system, or transmitted in any form or by any means,
electronic, electrostatic, magnetic tape, mechanical, photocopying, recording or otherwise,
without permission in writing from the publishers,
Gomer Press, Llandysul, Dyfed, Wales.

Printed at Gomer Press, Llandysul, Dyfed, Wales

Contents

Map of Swansea		vi
Foreword	Oliver Fairclough	vii
Acknowledgements		viii
Introduction		iv
The Pottery Site		v
Chapter 1	George Haynes at the Cambrian Pottery 1789-1810	1
Chapter 2	George Haynes and Lewis Weston Dillwyn.	4
Chapter 3	The establishment of the new Pottery	6
Chapter 4	Workforce	11
Chapter 5	Site Excavations	15
Chapter 6	The Wares	17
	GROUP I Creamware	18
	GROUP II Hand painted wares	19
	GROUP III Transfer printed wares	26
	GROUP IV Miscellaneous Wares	*45*
	SHAPES, MARKS, PRICES AND MEASURES	48
Chapter 7	The Haynes Family	75
Chapter 8	George Haynes's other interests in Swansea.	78
Chapter 9	The Ynystanglwys Estate	83
Epilogue		87
Selected Bibilography		88
Appendix I	Agreements	89
Appendix II	William Bryant's Workbook	90
Index to Illustrations of Wares		94

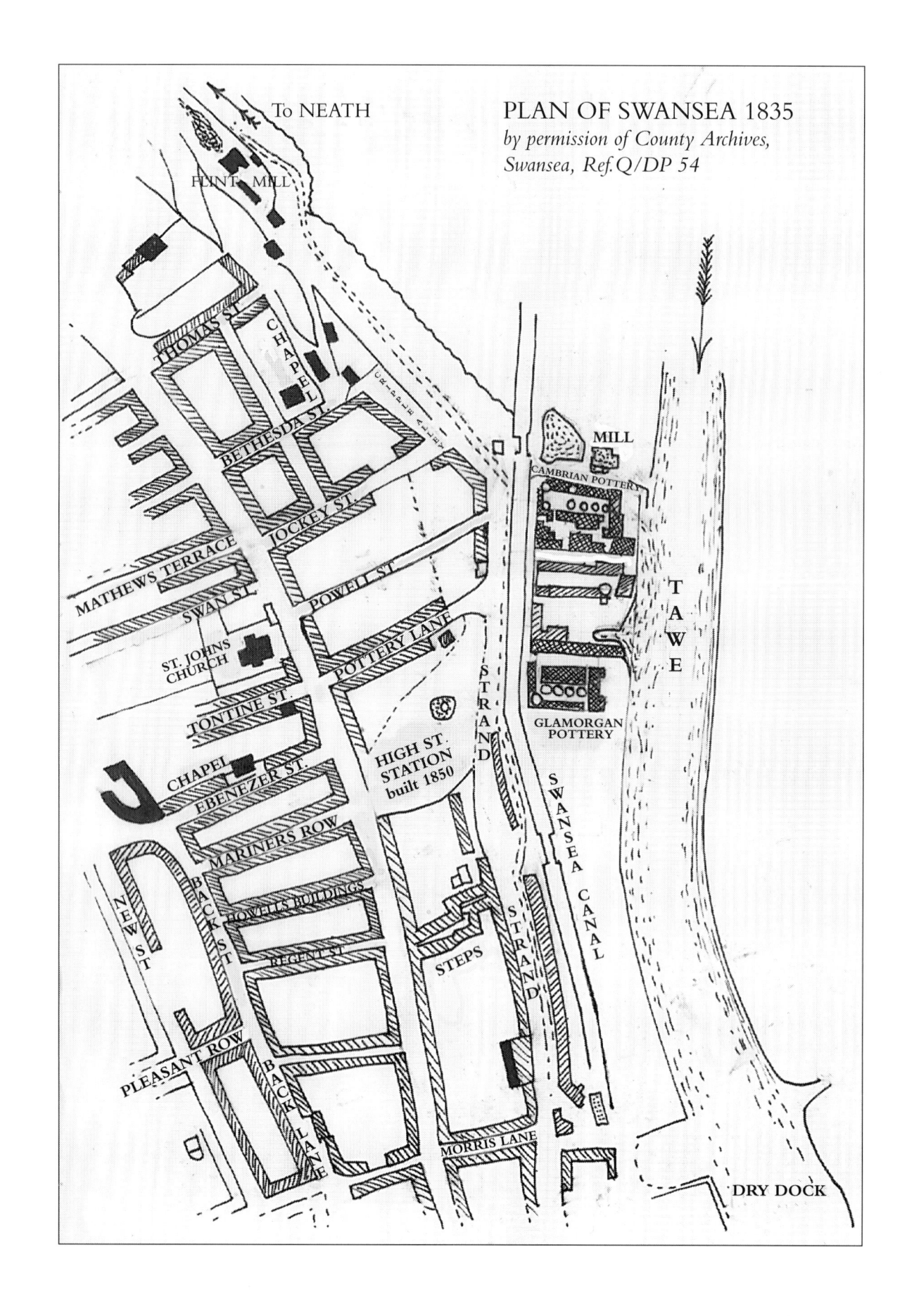

PLAN OF SWANSEA 1835
by permission of County Archives, Swansea, Ref. Q/DP 54

Foreword

The firm of Baker, Bevans and Irwin, proprietors of the Glamorgan Pottery, Swansea between 1814 and 1838, made good quality earthenwares during one of the most interesting periods of British ceramic history in which mass-production, improving technology and a burgeoning export market transformed the craft-based industry of the 18th century. With the publication of this book, the history of the Glamorgan Pottery is now better documented than many of its rivals in the Staffordshire Potteries, in Bristol, Liverpool and elsewhere. Helen Hallesy both tells its story and compiles a formidable record of the shapes and patterns used by it. The printed patterns found on the Pottery's tea, dinner and toilet wares, as well as those on the charming child's plates which it produced in surprisingly large numbers, reflect the changing tastes and popular concerns in South Wales, Ireland and the West of England during the reigns of George IV and William IV.

The story of the Glamorgan Pottery is an important part of the history of the pottery industry in South Wales, a history which extends from the founding of the Cambrian Pottery in 1764 to the final kiln firing at Llanelli in 1922. George Haynes is generally regarded as the man responsible for the very considerable success of the Cambrian Pottery between the early 1790s and 1810, and the impression is reinforced by what is revealed in this study of his achievement as founder of the Glamorgan, his subsequent venture.

The Glamorgan Pottery has hitherto been somewhat overshadowed by attention that collectors and specialists have paid to its larger neighbour and rival, the Cambrian Pottery. Now that neglect has been remedied by means of a volume which gives us much new information about the Glamorgan Pottery and its wares, in text and illustrations. There is no doubt that for all pottery enthusiasts, this book will be a source of information and much pleasure.

Oliver Fairclough
National Museums and Galleries of Wales

Acknowledgements

It gives me sincere pleasure to acknowledge and express my thanks and appreciation for the help and co-operation I have received from Museums and collectors in granting consent for their pottery to be photographed and illustrated in this book.

I am indeed indebted to the Swansea Museum (whose collections formerly belonged to the Royal Institution of South Wales, Swansea) and The Glynn Vivian Art Gallery, now both part of Swansea City Council Museum Service; also The National Museums and Galleries of Wales, Cardiff, with particular thanks to Oliver Fairclough for his time in checking the proofs. I would also like to thank the staff of the Swansea Library for their unending patience with reference enquiries; and South Glamorgan County Library, Cardiff, for their permission to print the note book on Glamorgan Pottery shapes, sizes and colour recipes.

Other friends who have given me assistance or pointed me in the right direction, particularly with enquiries of local interest are Michael Gibbs and Bernard Morris.

For their help and patience with the photography, I would like to thank Graham Matthews, Brian Sharp and Roberta Williams.

Above all, I would like to express my gratitude to Gomer Press for undertaking to publish this book, hereby bringing it to fruition.

Finally, but by no means least, are the friends and collectors who have generously allowed me to invade their homes or entrust me with their pieces of pottery for photograhy. I am greatly indebted to: Michael Benson, Roger Binney, Wyndham Bowen, Christopher Brown, John B. Davies, Wynford Edwards, Ieuan and Gwyneth Evans, Roderick Evans, Michael Foley, Derek Harper, Jan and William Mayberry, Howard Morgan, Andrew Nethercott, Donald Treharne, Eric Williams and Rowland Williams.

Helen Hallesy

Introduction

In 1942, Ernest Morton Nance, an Oxford graduate and former master of Classics at Swansea Grammar School, published a massive work entitled *The Pottery and Porcelain of Swansea and Nantgarw.* The author being a classical scholar, lawyer and ceramic authority, the book shows a deep knowledge of the chemistry of ceramics and explores thoroughly every aspect of the Swansea Potteries. It is a monumental work.

Nance had married a Miss S.L. Yeo, the daughter of a local industrialist who had purchased the site of the Cambrian Swansea pottery when it finally closed down in 1870. This connection, together with his wide interest in ceramics, led to his introduction to and eventual love of the products made at Swansea. His hobby expanded into an unending, challenging search for pieces, marked and unmarked, which he studied and documented over a period of many tireless years.

During his retirement, spent at his native St Ives in Cornwall, he undertook the arduous task of compiling material for his book. It is his work which has been such an inspiration to both researchers and collectors, and it is to him that so many of us are indebted. One of the chapters in his book is devoted to the Glamorgan Pottery and it is his text, therefore, which has laid the foundation stone for this study.

The products of the Glamorgan Pottery at Swansea have never been awarded the recognition or consideration that they deserve. For an establishment which was comparatively small in size, it achieved a perfection of potting and a range of decorative styles which could compete successfully with any other manufacturer in the country in the early nineteenth century. Sadly, the pottery has been neglected and scant attention paid to it in any literature relating to nineteenth century ceramics published during the last fifty years or so, possibly because the wares have not been particularly fashionable. Collectors of 'Swansea' have generally disregarded the minor Glamorgan Pottery in Swansea as being some distanced, far-removed establishment, without realising that it was, in fact, the next door neighbour of the famous Cambrian pot works.

The purpose of this book is to give an account of the historical background leading up to the establishing of the Glamorgan Pottery, and also to illustrate the vast range of patterns and designs which originated there and were, indeed, later copied by the Cambrian. It is a study that aims to redress the balance.

It was undoubtedly the outstanding abilities of George Haynes, its founder, who combined the abilities of craftsman and businessman, which made the venture a success in the face of fierce competition from the well established Cambrian and numerous Staffordshire potteries at that time. Much of the narrative of this book therefore focusses on George Haynes, his previous experience as manager of the Cambrian pottery and his reasons for leaving and creating a second pot works in the town: the Glamorgan Pottery, in 1814. His actions are also placed within the wider context of his other business ventures and his social life in Swansea and surrounding districts. Information about the early life of George Haynes, prior to arriving at Swansea, is sparse. As founder of the 'Cambrian' newspaper he had considerable editorial control and could censor any news relating to his private life. Consequently, little appears. Nevertheless, some new background information on this key figure did emerge during research, and will add to our understanding of the history.

Unlike the Cambrian or Llanelly potteries, the Glamorgan has no 'early', 'middle' or 'late' period. During its 24 years of production between 1814 and 1838, there was a consistency of high-quality, well-made wares, which fed a mainly local market in South Wales and the south-west coast of England. The Napoleonic war with France ended in 1815 and the subsequent opening-up of trade in the post-war period led to fierce competition between the major earthenware-producing potteries as the home market expanded to meet the demand for new designs. A competitive war raged for price, variety, designs and new ideas. It is hoped that this publication will provide collectors with detailed information on the wide range and high quality of ceramics achieved at the Glamorgan pottery during those years.

For myself, the research involved has proved both exciting and rewarding, with new discoveries never failing to fascinate. There will always be unanswered questions, pieces of the jigsaw left to find and fit, but it is hoped that at least some of the blank spaces can be filled, and that a study such as this helps us move a little closer towards completion of the picture.

The Pottery Site

The best illustration of the site on which the Glamorgan Pottery stood is to be found in a painting of circa 1818, attributed to Thomas Hornor. The watercolour shows a panoramic view of Swansea, looking west from Kilvey Hill. An enlarged section of the painting, reproduced with the kind permission of Swansea Museum, Swansea City Council, can be seen on the endpapers of this volume.

The two pottery sites can be seen clearly, adjacent to eachother, the Cambrian being dominated by seven bottle kilns on the northern (right hand) side, and a further two kilns, which were added in 1814, in the centre foreground of this view. To the extreme right of the Cambrian stands the pottery mill. The Glamorgan Pottery is bounded by the long, windowless wall running from east to west between the Strand and the river bank. The viewpoint from which the painting was executed tends to conceal the tops of the bottle kilns (four in all, according to the plan) which must have been situated between the long wall and the warehouses or buildings to the extreme south.

The potteries were separated only by a lane leading to the river Tawe. At the mouth of the long, grey building is an opening leading from the Pottery to the river bank, providing easy access for water transport on the large sailing vessels secured alongside the potteries. Behind both pottery sites runs the old Turnpike Road or Strand, which borders the fields running up to Swansea's High Street. Leading from the Cambrian Pottery up to High Street is Powell Street. A more extensive representation of Swansea's geography at the time is provided in the map on page vi.

Beaufort Place can be seen above and to the left of the Glamorgan Pottery site: it was demolished in the 1930s to make way for a railway turntable just below the frontage of High Street Station. The tall, three-storeyed house above it (pink in colour) is the house where George Haynes lived when he worked at the Cambrian Pottery prior to 1810. This is also shown on a sketch map of the Cambrian Pottery, 1802, to be found in Swansea Museum.

Chapter 1

GEORGE HAYNES AT THE CAMBRIAN

The history and background of the Glamorgan Pottery must begin with reference to the principal manufacturer of pottery in Swansea in the early nineteenth century—the Cambrian, which had stood on a site in the Strand since the early 1760s. Inevitably, the story of any industrial concern is rooted in the social, political and economic climate of the time, and the forty years of successful potting at the Cambrian prior to the erection of the Glamorgan Pottery in 1814 has an immediate link with the success of its rival.

Whilst it has always been recorded that William Coles of Cadoxton, Neath, founded the Cambrian Pottery, no reason is usually given for his decision to take an interest in business in South Wales, as he was at this time far removed from his original home in Gloucestershire. To trace this interest, we must begin with his father-in-law, Rowland Pytt.

In 1736 a lease was granted to Messrs. Rowland Pytt (of Gloucester) Morse and Lewis, for operating a forge and iron mill in the quiet hamlet of Clydach, near Swansea, an estate called Ynyspenllwych. It is possible that initially the forge worked to supply arms to Cromwell's ironsiders, but certainly, by the 1740s Ynyspenllwych was turning out tinplate—the first tinplate works in Glamorgan. In 1747 Rowland Pytt was also granted a lease by Lord Mansel for Melin-y-Court furnace, Neath, 'the tenant to pay 6d per dozen for all mines or iron ore that shall be raised on Lord Mansel's lands'. The rolling mills at Ynys-y-gerwin, Aberdulais were also built by or for the same Pytt of Gloucester in 1750. Pytt was therefore an established and substantial iron master of both Neath and Clydach forges.

The repercussions of the next turn of events were to be of the utmost significance in the history of potting at Swansea.

In 1753 Rowland Pytt the elder died and left in his will 'To my daughter Hannah, wife of William Coles, ironmonger of the city of Gloucester, all my shares and leases of the Roll Mill and Tinworks at Ynyspenllwych'. Coles and his wife also inherited Pytt's ironworks at Neath where it is recorded that 'a new partner in the form of William Coles came on the scene in the same period', (the year of Pytt's death).

Coles now found himself with an expanding iron and tinplate works at Clydach and Neath Abbey to manage and control, and from a considerable distance. Although he is referred to as 'Coles of Cadoxton' this was purely his business address, for he never left his home town of Gloucester, over a hundred miles away.

Within ten years his interests had widened, and in 1764 he took the historic step of opening, on a disused copperworks site in the Strand, Swansea, the first pottery works in that town. The development of the Cambrian Pottery, as it was later to be called, has been the subject of interest and fascination to many historians and collectors of ceramics, and its hundred years or so of successful potmaking is recorded in depth in the work of M. Nance referred to earlier.

Since William Coles never lived at Swansea and only occasionally gave supervision to the running of the pottery, he had little influence on it as a commercial business, delegating the management of it to a potter, probably one William Davies who supervised the day-to-day running of matters. During these early unprogressive years, there was little change or variety in the quality of the simple wares produced there.

On the death of William Coles in 1778, the estate, including the pottery, fell to his three sons who had no real interest in continuing the business of potting. By 1789 the old leases had been surrendered in favour of a new one to include John Coles (youngest son of William Coles of Gloucester) and a new partner, the new partner being one GEORGE HAYNES.

George Haynes was born in 1745, the son of George and Hannah Haynes. The family is documented (by Morton Nance) as being Quaker and having originated in Henley in Arden, Warwickshire. Certainly his tombstone in St. Mary's church yard, Swansea, records that his father was from Henley in Arden, Warwickshire, but I have been unable to trace George's birth place. Despite extensive research by archivists at Worcester and Warwick Record Office, no entries for the births or marriage of George and Hannah (father and mother),

1

or of George himself and his wife, Catherine, could be found. However, a copy of the will of George Haynes's father (b.1711) was found, in which he names his wife Hannah, daughter Hannah Ashwell, and sons George and James as beneficiaries. The other significant entry is in 1787, the birth and baptism of a daughter to George and Catherine, recorded at Warwick, St. Mary. This was their second daughter, Felicia, baptised on the twentieth of June 1787.

Had the family been Quakers, their marriages and births would have been listed in the International Genealogical Index—but nothing in Worcestershire, Warwickshire or Glamorgan was ever recorded. As Felicia was baptised in the Church of England, this seems rather to disprove the Quaker theory. There is some evidence to show the family had interests in the businesses of brewing and banking before coming to Swansea, although the reason for their removal to Wales is not clear. George Haynes's father, 'gentleman', an excise officer, died in 1784.

By 1789 George Haynes had arrived in Swansea with his widowed mother, Hannah, wife Catherine, and two daughters, Hannah aged eight and Felicia aged two. At forty five, George was now a mature businessman with a growing family. Although we know little of either George's early life or education, we can surmise that he was an educated man and that he had been engaged in businesses in the Warwick/Worcester area.

During the twenty years or so prior to Haynes's arrival at Swansea, the products of the Cambrian had been modest rough wares, saltglazed pieces with scratch blue decoration together with grey, white and cream coloured earthenwares with simple scratched or painted designs. Few pieces survive, but an excellent illustrated account can be found in Grant-Davidson's paper on 'Early Swansea Pottery 1764-1810' published in 1967.

The arrival of Haynes had an immediate impact. He joined the Swansea firm as a reliable partner and businessman who took immediate responsibility as manager. Haynes as we will see was a man of exceptional originality, of great imagination and foresight, coupled with a tremendous driving energy and enthusiasm for work. Although he lacked the working experience of a pottery or its technical processes, he had the confidence and capability of managing and developing successfully the operations within the Swansea potworks. No-one was to have a greater influence or impact on the history of potting at Swansea than Haynes.

John Coles, living in Gloucester, was far distanced from the pottery, and in his absence Haynes acted as sole proprietor and effected complete singular control of the business. There was an immediate injection of a new lease of life into the firm, and Haynes's responsibilities began with an extensive reorganisation of the pottery with more ambitious work attempted. By 1790, less than a year after his arrival, a sum in excess of £1,200 had been spent on new buildings. Potteries in Staffordshire had by now developed into large industries of first rate importance, due almost entirely to Josiah Wedgwood's inventive ideas and initiative—the genius of the industrial revolution in the potteries. At Etruria in Staffs, Wedgwood's highly successful business had proved an inspiration to Haynes, so much so that the Cambrian works were completely reorganised on similar lines to Wedgwood's factory. World-wide recognition had been gained by Wedgwood's Queensware or creamware, a fine cream coloured earthenware. The greatest form of flattery is imitation, and Haynes wasted no time in setting about trying to copy Wedgwood's designs and shapes. Creamware, caneware and black basalts were all imitated in body, colour and design. The development of transfer printing as a form of decoration opened up a market for cheaply produced quantities of attractive household wares, tea and dinner services, and toilet wares suitable for all tastes. Regrettably it is little appreciated that during this period Haynes produced his first experimental soft paste porcelain. Although inferior to the beautiful translucent porcelain which was later produced at the Cambrian, its production serves to illustrate the point that George Haynes was a man who was prepared to undertake the risk of attempting a new venture (amongst many others) in the name of expanding his potworks.

His working knowledge of experimental porcelain was later acknowledged by the decorator, William Weston Young, who had become involved in the newly established potworks at Nantgarw in 1814. Before committing himself to a partnership with Billingsley and

Walker, which involved financial payments, Young engaged the services of George Haynes to examine and report on the merits of the porcelain being produced at Nantgarw. Haynes's opinion was therefore highly valued and respected, he being probably the only man in South Wales with any experience in porcelain manufacture. For his investigative services, Young paid William Baker (Haynes's son-in-law, later to become manager of the Glamorgan pottery) on account of Haynes, the sum of three pounds. Haynes reported favourably and Young duly became a partner in the Nantgarw enterprise.

Between 1790-1791 Haynes conferred the title 'Cambrian' on the pottery, of which he was manager. This name was a popular one with him and was not confined to the pottery alone. He used it also for his 'Cambrian' brewery and later the 'Cambrian' newspaper. Once chosen, the name was retained by the pottery throughout its existance.

It was Haynes who was responsible for securing the services of many competant potters, painters and workmen at the Cambrian. Thomas Rothwell the engraver, George Bentley the modeller and Thomas Pardoe the decorator are some of the talented master craftsmen recruited. By now a larger workforce was needed to supply the increased demand for the quantity and variety of wares produced. Labour and materials would doubtless have been transported to Swansea from established pottery areas, and within a few years the Cambrian was well organised and running smoothly along the lines of Wedgwood's principles.

Invoices dated as early as April 1790 show that in a short time goods were successfully being produced and sold in great varieties. The next ten years saw a rapid expansion in the business, and impressive artistic achievements.

By 1800 John Coles had died, and on April the twenty first of that year, Coles's interest in the lease was passed on to George Haynes. The firm subsequently traded as 'Haynes and Co'.

In the monthly magazine or *British Register* of 1802 in an article reviewing Swansea as a progressive town, the writers comment that 'a stranger may expect to receive considerable satisfaction from visiting the Cambrian pottery most admirably conducted by Mr Haynes and his partners'. Also that year the *Swansea Guide* stated that 'the Cambrian pottery cannot fail to be an agreeable morning's amusement to those unacquainted with this form of manufacture—the concern has long been carried on by Mr Haynes to whose public spirit the town of Swansea is much indebted'.

In letters written during a *Tour through South Wales in 1803 and other times* the author referred to the pottery as being 'managed under the auspices of the ingenious Mr Haynes'. The pottery was therefore to all intents and purposes 'Haynes's pottery'.

Haynes had certainly fired the imagination of the people with new ideas and inspirational plans. His enthusiasm, vitality and hard work resulted in complete diversification of products and a resultant highly successful and competitive working pottery. He must be credited with not only the best management skills, but of having the foresight and confidence in his ability to place the Swansea potworks amongst the leading pottery manufacturers of Britain. On his shoulders rested all of the responsibility for manufacturing and marketing the new products at Swansea. He did not fail.

It can be said that the excellent range of ceramics attained at the Cambrian during the 1790-1810 period under Haynes's watchful eye was never surpassed. It must also be remembered that at this time, the close of the eighteenth and beginning of the nineteenth century, England was engaged in battle with France. War with Napoleon had resulted in depressed businesses in all sectors, low wages, high taxation and little or no export market. Pottery, as a luxury, was one of the first businesses to suffer, and yet Haynes during this period succeeded in accomplishing the finest potting ever achieved at Swansea.

Chapter 2

GEORGE HAYNES AND LEWIS WESTON DILLWYN

One of the most fascinating aspects in the background to the evolution of the Glamorgan pottery is the relationship that existed between the principal characters involved in its conception. Without George Haynes, the idea of the Glamorgan pottery would never have evolved, but without L. W. Dillwyn, Haynes would never have had the detemination or the will to ensure its success. The personalities of these men and their association must therefore be worthy of serious consideration as their roles as players in the drama of the history of this enterprise are of the utmost importance.

The earliest connection of L. W. Dillwyn with Swansea was the purchase of the Cambrian pottery by his father, William Dillwyn, in the hope that this would prove a profitable business for him. W. Dillwyn's second visit and inspection of the Cambrian in 1801 resulted in a new partnership. W. Dillwyn felt that the business would provide his son, Lewis, with an agreeable, worthwhile interest, and to this end he took over the pottery leases for the remainder of their term. He also purchased a major interest in the pottery itself, which cost him £13,000. The Dillwyn family was a wealthy one. William Dillwyn's diaries record that the family had owned and enjoyed large residencies in America before settling in Ipswich and his tour through England was taken in a leisurely way, without worrying about the cost on his return. Large amounts of cash were always available to Lewis for any venture he thought worthy as a business enterprise.

On instructions from William Dillwyn, therefore, Haynes took the son, L. W. Dillwyn, under his wing and was requested to 'use and exert his best interest and ability in favour of the pottery'. For his services, which he so ably executed, he was to receive the profits on three tenths of the business while young Dillwyn took the remaining seven tenths. It is no surprise that this financial arrangement, together with the disparity in ages (Haynes was fifty-seven, Dillwyn twenty-four) was to result in friction.

In 1802 the firm of Haynes, Dillwyn and Co. came into existence. Dillwyn was a gifted naturalist and his past years had been devoted to this cause. His specialist knowledge of botany was to make a lasting contribution to the science of plants and also greatly influenced his ideas for new designs on the ceramics at Swansea.

Haynes had spent fourteen years in the pottery business and was aquainted with every managerial detail, including the staffing, technical and commercial aspects at the Cambrian. He was more than old enough to be Dillwyn's father. He resided in High Street, a few yards from the pottery, and was on site should any problem arise, while Dillwyn lived temporarily at Burrows Lodge, a little distance away. For all of these reasons, the arrival of Dillwyn had no immediate effect on the management, Haynes continuing to run the business authoritatively and independently while Dillwyn had everything to learn.

In 1807 Dillwyn married Mary Llewellyn of Penllergaer and became a most active trustee in his father-in-law's large estate. Furthermore, from 1802 to 1809 he was preoccupied with writing and publishing his botanical work, *The British Confervae* which helped elect him as a fellow of the Royal Society and Linnaen Society. Dillwyn's interest in the pottery could not therefore have occupied his full attentions or interests during these early years, at least not as his father might have hoped. Dillwyn's influence was seen, however, in one particular direction. In 1803, he engaged the services of William Weston Young, a fellow friend, naturalist, and ceramic decorator, to provide illustrations for his work. A versatile and talented painter, Young was responsible for the noted Swansea services decorated with butterfly and bird subjects. His work was in the nature of special commissions for Dillwyn as a friend and not on a commercial basis. Thomas Pardoe, the principal decorator at the pottery was also directed to copy flower paintings from Curtis's *Botanical Magazine*, with named specimens written on the reverse of the piece. These botanical paintings together with the bird and animal subjects after Bewick, and other shell and seaweed designs, clearly show Dillwyn's influence on designs. The work contributed by these two men within the 1802-1808 period under the guidance of Dillwyn have proved to be some of the most desirable of all hand painted pieces executed at the pottery. Some services, notably the butterfly paintings, would have been produced for Dillwyn's personal pleasure and not for resale.

Dillwyn's limited influence on mainstream pottery procedures was, perhaps, no fault of his own, as Haynes retained his superior managerial position. Although Dillwyn was financially the chief partner, no work was executed without direction or advice from Haynes. Furthermore, although it is known that Haynes instructed his new partner in many of the workings of the pottery, it is also clear that he was disinclined to impart all the working knowledge of his years. In 1820, during a long and complicated court case involving Dillwyn and the new firm of Bevington and Co., Dillwyn, although by no means predisposed in Haynes's favour, said of him, (Bill and Answer filed in Chancery Court of 1821) 'it must be remembered that George Haynes the elder is the person who originally built the greater part, and for many years before, had entirely managed the Pottery, and from whom in 1802 it was purchased by my father and for more than 7 years afterwards continued to be its manager and taught me all I knew of the business'. However, Haynes was inclined on occasion to withhold information and only told Dillwyn what he wished and no more, therefore hindering his learning process. The numerous experiments which Haynes conducted on soaprock, used in the production of porcelain, were well guarded secrets and Haynes was obviously reluctant to share his ideas with his new partner. During their early partnership Dillwyn was sent to Cornwall on Haynes's instructions, to obtain a supply of soaprock for the pottery without being given any explanation as to its intended use. Dillwyn would doubtless have resented such a mean gesture.

Their partnership therefore could not have been a happy one, since it lacked trust and confidence. Yet at the end of the agreed seven year term of partnership, Dillwyn was not ready to take on full responsibility for the business and extended the term for a further nine months, to expire in March 1810.

After twenty one years service at the Cambrian, Haynes terminated his agreement with Dillwyn, his departure being accompanied by that of his assistant and son-in-law, William Baker (Hannah's husband). This did not worry Haynes financially as he was a banker in the town with a rapidly growing business, (see Chapter 8) ran a successful brewery with his son George, and was engaged in many public affairs. Haynes spent little time at the Cambrian during his last eight or nine months employment and became quite detached from the business affairs— visiting only once on March 9, 1810, to determine a valuation of the stock and his share of the profits. His concern was for his son-in-law, William Baker, who now found himself without employment.

Haynes, obviously resentful at being compelled to leave the pottery at the height of its success, gained mainly through his own achievements, now entered into a most dishonourable scheme to annoy and alienate Dillwyn. His banking partner Henry Pocklington and friends Messrs. Hendrie and Co., Brewers, were persuaded to purchase the buildings adjacent to the Cambrian pottery on Haynes's behalf. Unbeknown to Dillwyn and whilst still in partnership with him, Haynes installed and erected the machinery for making 'SOAP' in the very heart of the pottery buildings. His new unsavoury business was announced in the *Cambrian* on March 24th: 'The public are respectfully informed that soap is now ready for delivery at the above works. Captains of vessels trading to different parts in the channel will find great advantages in this establishment.' An unendurable smell arose immediately after work commenced, which moved Dillwyn swiftly into action. It led to court proceedings against Haynes's conduct 'in setting up such an objectionable manufactory against his partner'. Dillwyn rejoiced in the court's decision to have the soap works closed down, and although only awarded £10 in damages, Dillwyn succeeded in embarrassing George Haynes into paying £1,200 in costs. His conduct had been unbecoming of a gentleman who hitherto had been regarded with respect and loyalty.

This very public affair led to a miserable breakdown in their relationship, Dillwyn feeling betrayed and losing all trust in Haynes. The situation smouldered and finally led to both men refusing to speak to one another.

It was after the trial in September 1810 that Haynes set about his new idea of establishing a competitive pottery in direct opposition to his former partner. From a failed partnership and much public acrimony, a new determination developed in George Haynes, and plans were thus hatched for the formation of the Glamorgan Pottery. Although Haynes's name never appears in the title of the Pottery firm, and he never actually became a partner, it was undeniably his idea which led to its conception, and he who financed it. The scheme took several years to reach completion, as Haynes's time became preoccupied with the building of a new residence at Clydach—completed in 1811 (see Chapter 9) followed by the death of his wife, Catherine, in October of that year. But within three years, the building of the kilns, workshops, storehouses and offices, together with the installation of new plant, was complete.

The Glamorgan Pottery was to be the final chapter in the pottery career of George Haynes.

Chapter 3

THE ESTABLISHMENT OF THE NEW POTTERY

The idea of the Glamorgan Pottery as a rival to the Cambrian in Swansea was conceived by Haynes and went ahead under his direction and with his capital. He was responsible for its inception and it was his bank in Wind St., Swansea, which financed it. Yet the role he chose to play at the Glamorgan was as the man behind the scenes, the advisor in times of difficulty, the guiding spirit, the person who gave the factory a firm grounding. It seems ironic that the Glamorgan Pottery factory mark bears the names of Baker, Bevans and Irwin, none of whom were potters or had any working knowledge of a pottery, and that Haynes chose to omit his name from the standard mark. Few early examples of pottery bear his impressed 'H' mark. (See Pl.167). It was quite obvious then, as now, that it was Haynes's skill, experience and well known ability in pottery management that attracted the Bevans and induced them to participate in this new business venture.

The new pottery buildings were erected on a site which lay about half way up 'The Strand' in Swansea, a road which ran for about a mile along the side of the river Tawe—a busy thoroughfare especially for traffic connected with shipping and general merchandise. The new factory now lay adjacent to the older Cambrian and was separated from it only by a lane leading to the river bank. The canal ran along the Western side of both potteries, dividing the works from the road. Flint and other materials were ground at a mill situated at Landore, several miles up the valley, and subsequently transported back to the pottery along the canal. Although the pottery might have been trading as early as 1813, it was not until the year of 1814 that it became active.

The site of the new pottery was well positioned on the banks of the Tawe, approached through sheltered water. Clay-bearing vessels from Devon and Cornwall could easily navigate the waters and tie-up alongside the works. The cost of land transport made it virtually impossible for inland movement of raw materials to the pottery and finished products out of it. Swansea, along with many other coastal settlements, looked to the sea for transport of their exports and imports. Thus shipping links with the south-west coast of England became well established, with raw clay being exchanged for coal.

The first half of the nineteenth century saw the 'take-off' of Swansea in its development as an industrial centre and port of international importance. By the end of the nineteenth century Swansea had been transformed into not only a town of industrial wealth, but also urban culture and tourism. From a small town of 6,000 in 1801, the population of Swansea grew to 13,000 in 1833. It was during this period of sudden and dramatic expansion that the Glamorgan Pottery was founded. The site leased comprised 'part of the Bank, being 35 yards in breadth from the wall built by Alexander Raby Esq. on the North, and 98 yards (including the Swansea Canal) from the Turnpike Road to the line marked by the Swansea Harbour Trustees for general embankment of the river, situated and being on the Strand in Swansea. The premises and buildings have been erected by the lessees and the premises are now called THE GLAMORGAN POTTERY'.

The lessees were WILLIAM BAKER of Swansea; WILLIAM BEVAN and WILLIAM BEVAN the younger, of Morriston; ROBERT BEVAN of Monmouth; MARTIN BEVAN of Risca and THOMAS IRWIN of Swansea, six gentlemen in all.

Initially the lease was for a term of sixty years, at £5 per annum, which was approved by the Corporation, although this lease was subsequently surrendered for a new lease in 1816. The second lease was changed to a term of ninety years at an annual rent of £20 per annum for the first twenty three years, and £60 per annum for the residue of the term. The pottery would trade as 'THE GLAMORGAN POTTERY AND CO'. These six men became the new partners in a business association with George Haynes, although his name never appeared as a partner. The capital of the company was divided into twelve parts or shares namely:

    William Baker holding 3 twelfths
    William Bevan, 2 twelfths
    William Bevan the younger, 1 twelfth
    Robert Bevan 2 twelfths
    Martin Bevan 2 twelfths
    Thomas Irwin 2 twelfths.

The proprietors undertook to erect buildings appropriate to the manufacture of china and earthenware and agreed to spend the sum of £3,000 on appropriate buildings.

The BEVANS of Morriston were all related. William Bevan senior had three sons, Martin, Robert, and William, also two daughters, one of whom, Elizabeth, married Thomas Irwin in 1804.

William Bevan the elder and sons Robert and William were already partners in the Landore Iron Company at Morriston while William the younger and Martin were patentees and actively engaged in a new copper smelting process. In 1794 the Swansea Harbour Trustees had ordered a contract with William Bevan (the elder) of Morriston 'to build the Pier (Western) at the entrance to the Harbour in the port' and again in 1802 he was commissioned to cost for 'the building of the Eastern Pier, the deepening of the Bar and the erection of Gates for impounding the water in the river'. He was a man of much experience in the iron and copper industry, being the 'head copper man' in the former Morris firm at Landore.

The Nantrhyd-y-Vilais works had been established by the Bevans at Landore in or around the year 1805 and were erected on the brook of that name to the north of the tinplate works. They were 'air furnaces of an exceptional character, neither for copper nor iron and yet for both'. The Bevans' hope was to extract copper from the slags which, it was supposed, had not been smelted with sufficient care, and also to extract the iron which was known to form a proportion of at least 50% of the slag. The result was a scientific success but although a little copper was reclaimed and iron was rolled out at the mills, it was found to be impossible to 'weld' and so remained unmarketable. The proprietors came to grief, the works were closed and the problem of extracting a marketable iron from the millions of tons of slag remained a problem. Penny copper tokens were issued in 1813 which read on the obverse side 'Nantrhydyvilas Air Furnace Co.' and on the reverse 'Payable at Swansea, Morriston 1813'.

In 1816 the firm became founders of brass and iron and were also makers of edge tools and shovels. At Landore the mills had supplied iron tinplates to the

Oystermouth Railway Company at Swansea, the first passenger railway in Britain.

Undoubtedly, the Bevans of Morriston, as entrepreneurs, had experienced both success and failure and were tempted to any new business venture which promised lucrative rewards. It is also clear that the Bevan family had no working knowledge of a pottery and must have been drawn to it as a business venture purely on the recommendations and reputation of Haynes. One of the sons, Robert, was a doctor of medicine and lived at Monmouth. He seems to have been involved in name only in the new partnership, spending little or no time in Swansea.

THOMAS IRWIN was born in 1778 and must have had considerable sea going experience before being recruited at the age of 26 as 'Master' of the *Morriston*—a sloop hired by The Royal Navy between April 1804 and September 1812.

Described in the ship's muster as 'stout, 5ft. 8ins. high with fair complexion, dark hair, single and belonging to Swansea', Irwin remained in command of the *Morriston* until his retirement in 1812. The vessel was owned by Mr. John Morris of Clasemont, Morriston, Swansea and the Misses Bevan (William Bevan the elder's daughters).

Swansea shipping was now under threat and suffering considerable damage from French privateers. By April 1804 Captain Thomas Irwin was in command of the *Morriston*—a 2 masted sailing vessel intended for commercial trade and capable of delivering to the most remote creeks and beaches, and providing an essential and economical delivery service for many small coastal and river villages. Armed, and ready for naval duties, she patrolled the south-west corner of England, roughly between Plymouth and Swansea. Her two main bases were Stonehouse Poole (between Plymouth and Devonport) and the Mumbles Head. On her patrols she is recorded as often calling at Falmouth, Ilfracombe and occasionally the Scilly Islands. The patrols were probably an anti-invasion precaution as Napoleon was known to be massing ships in French ports.

Thomas Irwin's introduction to the Glamorgan Pottery was indirect. In 1804 he married Elizabeth Bevan, daughter of William Bevan of Morriston. His retirement as Captain in 1812 enabled him to involve himself in this new business venture which was taking place with the Bevan family and Haynes. Although Irwin took no active part in the new Pottery business, his name appears as one of the partners in the new firm of the Glamorgan Pottery, and was to remain with it until its closure. Sadly he was to remain a partner for only a few years; he died in February 1819 at the age of 42. In his will, he appointed Robert Bevan, doctor, of Avonmouth, and William Bevan the younger of Morriston (brothers-in-law) as executors and entrusted his real and personal estate to them as a means of providing an annual income for his wife, Elizabeth, and 6 dependent children. His assets, including his shares in the pottery, amounted to less than £800.00. Elizabeth Irwin took her husband's place as shareholder after 1819 and retained the name of Irwin throughout the life of the pottery.

The nominal head of the Glamorgan was WILLIAM BAKER, who held the largest portion of shares. William had married George Haynes's daughter, Hannah, in 1809, and had worked as Haynes's assistant at the Cambrian for several years. Of the six gentlemen in this new partnership, Baker was the only member with any working knowledge of pottery management and his abilities and experience, therefore, were crucial to the success of the Glamorgan.

It is interesting to note that the output from the Glamorgan pottery resulted in a dramatic increase in export sales of earthenware from Swansea. Whereas in 1812 the number of pieces of earthenware carried on vessels out of the port numbered 50,993, by 1819 the number amounted to 140,280 pieces, almost three times as many! It is known that after Haynes's departure from the Cambrian, business seems to have been almost at a standstill.[1] The following years, between 1811-17, were poor and unproductive for the Cambrian pottery under the management of Dillwyn and his new partners, the Bevingtons.

These export figures are therefore a clear indication of success, not at the Cambrian, but the smaller Glamorgan Pottery.

William Baker's period of control was to last a mere five years. His career ended in the year 1819 when he died, aged 47. The *Cambrian* newspaper of June 19th of that year records:

> Mr William Baker, one of the proprietors of the Glamorgan pottery in Swansea, whose memory will not cease to be cherished while worth and excellence are held in remembrance.

His death must have been felt deeply by the firm which had now lost its senior partner. Help came in the form of Hannah, Haynes's daughter, who took over her husband's interests and shares while retaining his name of Baker in the firm. Doubtless, Haynes would have been called upon to offer his services and advice at this time.

The responsibility for the pottery, however, now passed to the Bevan family. Nance records that Martin Bevan, aged 38, took control and became more practically interested in the pottery business. He held this managerial position until the closure of the factory in 1838. Over the next ten years or so, the pottery achieved much success in its development of new shapes and designs which continued to find an ever ready local market. This was perhaps surprising, because of the six original share holders, only the four Bevans remained, all of whom were preoccupied at this time with other business interests. The singular factor which cemented the factory together, directing and advising from the shadows, was Haynes. The Glamorgan had become a successful competitor. Haynes's capacity for engendering new business was obvious: he knew the products, knew the market. Although ageing (he was 75 in 1820) he not only kept the pottery in business, but made it flourish.

The significant event which directly precipitated the eventual closure of the Glamorgan was the failure of the Bevans firm in Morriston. By December 1829, William Bevan senior, William Bevan junior and Robert Bevan, co-partners in the Landore Iron Company, were forced to close down their foundry and were declared bankrupt. The late 1820s had been a depressed time for the iron trade generally, the country having gone through a severe depression. The Landore Iron Co. creditors forced the company to settle all outstanding accounts between them and their solvent partners in the Glamorgan pottery and were ordered to sell or dispose of their shares in the buildings and stock, either by auction or public sales.

On March 6th. of 1830, the *Cambrian* newspaper announced the disposal of five twelfths interest in the buildings and stock 'of that long established and lucrative Pottery concern in the town of Swansea, called the Glamorgan Pottery.' (William Bevan Snr. and Jnr. and Robert Bevan's shares). The offer was repeated three months later and again in November of that year:

> The pottery is in full work, on a very extensive scale, under the very superior management of one of the solvent partners, whose services will be continued.

The solvent partner was Martin Bevan.

As profits had decreased from the years 1827-30, the Bevans would have been quite happy to accept any reasonable offer for their shares at this time.

William Weston Young, who had been engaged at the Cambrian Pottery as ceramic artist for several years from 1803 and who later had become involved in financially assisting Billingsley and Walker in 1814 in establishing their small pottery at Nantgarw in order to produce porcelain, had been left in a position of bankruptcy as a result of his generosity. His enthusiasm and interest, however, had not wavered as he continued to help his friends after their removal to Swansea. Young's optimism and faith in the idea that a porcelain of exceptional quality and remarkable translucency could successfully be produced in South Wales did not falter, so much so that years later in 1832 he was still of the opinion that the idea was a feasible one and consulted with Mr Martin Bevan (March 1832), Hannah Baker and William Woodward-Haynes, 'on the subject of The Glamorgan Pottery' with a view to taking the lease and trying out his new recipes.

In 1832, May 2nd, he collected some pieces of porcelain which he had given to Martin Bevan to be biscuit fired. The entry in his diary reads: 'Had the pieces of china from M. Bevan' and the following day he called at the Glamorgan Pottery and noted 'Fire'd up the heat of the biscuit kiln, not sufficient for this body'. These porcelain trials of his continued for several months but sadly Young's dreams never materialised, his plans never reached fruition. Young eventually abandoned the idea.

Coincidentally, as the life of the pottery seemed to be drawing to a close, George Haynes died in the January of 1830, at his home in Clydach, aged 85 years.

His obituary which appeared in the *Cambrian* of Jan. 9th was richly deserved. He had been a forceful man of energy, decision, with a great aptitude for business, who had educated his children into the businesses of potting, brewing and banking. The notice showed an exceptional respect for his person and his achievements.

> Died, on Saturday last, in his eighty-fifth year, George Haynes Esquire, whose memory will long be revered by his relatives and all who knew him. For the last forty years of his life, this venerable gentleman was a resident in Swansea or its neighbourhood, and during a great part of that period his efforts were exerted to benefit the trade of the town. To him we are indebted for the establishment of the first earthenware pottery, whose manufacture has now become a staple commodity, and under his auspices and support, this paper—The first published in Wales—was started. Indeed the earlier part of his life was a scene of active industry and utility, and his character was at once marked by strict integrity and unostentatious liberality.

He was buried at St. Mary's church, Swansea, where his gravestone can still be seen.

The five twelfths shares held by the Bevans were purchased by Martin Bevan and son, Thomas, but sadly, there was no injection of new blood into the quietly declining pottery. The death of George Haynes was closely followed by that of Hannah in 1835, events which appear to have left the pottery bereft of its strengths. At some point during these latter years, Samuel Fox Parsons (Haynes's son in law, married to Felicia, his youngest daughter) and William Woodward Haynes (Haynes's youngest son), joined the firm, taking over Hannah's share and retaining the Haynes family interest.

The Pottery languished in the hands of further inexperienced partners joining the business. How desperate the position had become by 1837 can be appreciated by the decision of the co-partners to meet with L.W. Dillwyn and son, with a view to selling out to their arch rivals. The meeting, held late in 1837, proved irrevocable. Martin Bevan, representing the Glamorgan, agreed the sale of the Glamorgan and all its stock to the Dillwyns.

Lewis Llewellyn Dillwyn's interest in acquiring the Glamorgan was with the view solely to closing it down and putting an end to its competitive business. It seemed that there was not enough work to keep both potteries fully occupied and that the Cambrian was sufficiently large enough to manufacture and supply earthenware to meet every possible demand placed on it. The truth of the matter was that the Dillwyns had regarded Haynes's business as a thorn in their side for long enough, and were only too happy to have been placed in a position of terminating their long suffered business. They must have rejoiced in the year 1838 which proved to be the last for the Glamorgan. The eventual elimination of the opposing Glamorgan Pottery did not, however, end Dillwyn's problems. Ever increasing competition from the Staffordshire potteries, where superior earthenwares were being produced, continued to make life difficult and a more threatening local rival arose in the form of the newly emerging pottery at Llanelli. Much of the Glamorgan machinery and some moulds, notably jugs, were purchased by William Chambers Junior of Llanelli, for his new works. These, together with some of the workforce, who took with them years of experience, meant that the new South Wales Pottery had a 'headstart'. From its inception, the pottery at Llanelli became yet another fierce threat to the Cambrian, particularly in supplying the local Welsh market. It progressed rapidly and successfully, so much so that it proved to be a major contributory factor in the eventual closure of the Cambrian some years later in 1868.

By December 1838 therefore, the Glamorgan Pottery had closed its doors. In May of the following year, 1839, an announcement appeared in the Cambrian advertising the sale of its stock of earthenware:

> consisting of Dinner and Dessert Services, Chamber sets and Tea sets, Jugs, Mugs and Bowls, with a great variety of other articles and are now selling off by Private Contract, at a reduction of 20% below the regular prices

and again the following September :

> To sell by Auction on the premises, on Monday, September 23rd 1839, and following days, until the whole is disposed of, the remaining stock in Trade.

The demise of the Glamorgan pottery heralded the end of an era in which George Haynes had been the central protagonist, the inspiration and influence on all around him. His contribution to the efficiency and success of his undertaking was second to that of no other person. The results of his achievements in the early nineteenth century have provided the source for a rewarding field of study and collecting. The name of Dillwyn has always been regarded as synonymous with Swansea pottery: as knowledge of the contribution made by George Haynes becomes more widespread, his name too may rank equally in the history of pottery manufacture of the town.

Note 1: The arrival of Samuel Walker and William Billingsley at Swansea in 1814 had drawn Dillwyn's attentions to the manufacture of porcelain with which he became preoccupied. Numerous experimental trials followed, aimed at perfecting a commercially viable porcelain of superior translucency. This work, coupled with the death of his father-in-law in July 1817, accounted for Dillwyn's withdrawal from the pottery business and his subsequent sale of his interest in the Cambrian pottery and 'China Works'.

Chapter 4

WORKFORCE

Undoubtedly one of the key men employed at the Glamorgan Pottery was WILLIAM BRYANT, clerk, potter, and later business agent for the pottery. Born in Bristol in 1792, it is possible that Bryant might have gained some experience of the pottery industry in one of the old Bristol potteries before moving to Swansea. He was certainly working at the Cambrian as early as 1811, then aged 19 years. Invoices made out to the Rev. John Collins of Oxwich for purchases of earthenware are recorded and signed by him in that year.

It is probable that Bryant would have worked under George Haynes at the Cambrian in his early years, whilst serving his pottery apprenticeship—he seems also to have been educated in the business of clerical work and accounting. Whatever his exact initial status, at some point after 1812, perhaps when the Glamorgan Pottery became viable, Bryant decided to join his old master in the setting up of his new establishment.

The importance of skilled workmen cannot be over-emphasised, the pottery being only as good as its potters and decorators. Many of the old workforce who had doubtless developed their careers under Haynes's wing, would have remained loyal to him, their old master, and taken up their new duties with him in preference to working with the younger Dillwyn who had spent little time with the workers between his arrival in 1802 and Haynes's departure in 1810. In 1807, for example, following his marriage to Mary, (daughter of John Llewellyn of Penllergaer) at Piccadilly, London, Dillwyn had not resided in Swansea for a whole year.

Bryant, along with other workmen, would not have left the Cambrian forcibly as Haynes and William Baker had done, but out of free choice on their parts. William Bryant remained as potter, overseer and business representative for the Glamorgan Pottery until its closure in 1838 when he left to take up the post of manager of the new Llanelly Pottery works.

Quite by chance, I recently discovered an important note book, apparently lost for many years, its significance never being realised.[1] The writing has been identified as that of Bryant's hand, most of the notes in it having been recorded while he was still employed at the Glamorgan Pottery in 1838. They make fascinating reading. (Some of the pages are reproduced by the kind permission of the South Glamorgan County Library as Appendix II.)

The covers of the note book are missing, as are its first pages, so it begins with a table listing: 'Sizes of the ware made at the Glamorgan Pottery December 22nd. 1838'.

A bewildering diversity in the number of shapes and sizes of items produced in the pottery follows, from bowls, ('gallon, pudding, grecian') to chamber pots, chair pans, cups, ewers, coffee cans, pots, trifle cans, vases, jelly moulds, mustard pots, jugs, peppers, patty pans, mugs, etc. Sadly, many of the interesting shapes listed here have never been found on known Glamorgan patterns—but one can only hope!

It is reasonable to assume that the book was designed as a working reference book—the measurements presumably the dimensions to which the thrower needed to work. Contraction in the biscuit kiln would reduce the piece to its final trade size. The figures were never meant for publication, being used solely for domestic reference and identification.

An experienced, knowledgeable man, Bryant had spent the best working years of his life in the potteries (27 years) during which time he and his colleagues had learned by trial and error, to perfect recipes for glazes and coloured enamels, the best methods of manipulating the materials, of controlling kiln atmosphere and determining firing temperatures. Many other details, once discovered, were precisely recorded and put in safe keeping.

Pages of recipes for 'Glamorgan Pottery Glazes etc' follow, together with comprehensive notes listing chemical ingredients for the making of colours. The following is a summary of the colours listed, (See also Appendix II)

'Orange under glaze'
'To prepare tin ashes for yellow'
'To prepare blue for Common Green colour'
'Common Green'
'White enamel'
'A further Enamel Green'
'Enamel Black'
'Flux for enamel Yellow'
'Enamel Blue'
'Edging Green'
'Pink colour'
'Another edging Green'
'Chrome Yellow'
'To make matt Blue'
'French Green'
'Victoria Green'
'Torque Stain'

Precise, detailed measured ingredients are included, together with instructions for the position during firing e.g. 'at the top' or 'at the bottom' of the appropriate kiln, in order to obtain the correct temperature to develop the colour. Although variations in raw materials were always a problem, wide differences in the various proportions were acceptable, as success depended upon the methods of making and particularly the method of firing—this was the art.

Exact diagrams and drawings of biscuit and gloss kilns with precise measurements (presumably for their reconstruction at The Llanelly Pottery) are also recorded.

Such information would be known only to a minimum of persons; here were jealously guarded trade secrets, kept only by the master or trusted custodian. As the month of December 1838 was a time when the pottery was approaching closure, one can only speculate that Bryant was recording permanently, for the last time, the formulae, proportions of ingredients and 'tips' which were as important as the recipes themselves.

The book gives a fascinating account of information which could be 'sold', as was the case for a 'Pink Colour' recipe;

18th. of Oxide of Tin
9 of Whitening
1 of Chrome Yellow—mixed together and fired on top of Biscuit Kiln, then grind for use,—the above Mr Dillwyn gave £2 for it very freely.

Bryant was obviously not above selling a secret to the Cambrian Pottery next door for a decent price!

There are several recipes for 'frit', 'slip' and 'glaze',

also 'best glaze', the composition of which would have varied with the particular batch of firings—the composition of a good, reliable glaze often being a matter of difficulty, having to be neither too hard nor too soft.

The value of Bryant's experience was reflected in the hiring of him as business manager at the newly emerging South Wales Pottery works at Llanelli in the following year, 1839 (although he did not actually commence work until 1840). That he was a person of consequence is made clear by the acceptance of his managerial skills—at Llanelli he was given complete charge of the day to day workings of the new pottery.

There seems to be an interval in the pages of the book which would account for Bryant's departure from Swansea and, although not dated, the evidence suggests that the latter pages were written after his removal to Llanelli, one of his recipes being for 'the best glaze I made at Llanelly' (probably 1840).

22 China Clay		
48 Stone		The glaze is made as
18 Flint	Fritt	follows to every 120th of
18 Carbonate of Lime		the above fritt, add 20th
Borax		of the White Lead and
		3oz Blue calc. for stain

The similarity between the fine quality pottery produced at the Llanelly during the early William Chambers period 1840-55 and that of the Glamorgan is obviously a reflection of Bryant's experience and influence.

In addition to working at the Glamorgan, Bryant had by the year 1830 acquired his own lending library, a property in Calvert Street, Swansea (which then ran alongside St. Mary's Church) the contents of which were advertised for sale in the Cambrian newspaper of 27th June 1840:

> Sale at Swansea Library, Calvert St. 3rd July 1840.
> All the remaining household furniture of W. Bryant who is about to leave Swansea

The earliest mention of his library, which was attached to a stationer's premises and known as 'The Swansea Library' is in 1830—essentially commercial in nature, existing to provide a secondary income for its proprietor, while performing a service of social and cultural benefit to its customers.

Bryant left the Glamorgan Pottery, together with a nucleus of workmen, to take up new appointments at Llanelli during the year of 1840. Here he remained for a number of years before retiring to his home town of Bristol. In the 1861 census, his occupation is recorded as that of 'Merchant'. Bryant died at his home on June 9th 1867 at Queen's Square, aged 75.

Other known workers at the pottery are those recorded on the contract forms or 'Agreements' made between the pottery proprietors and its workmen (See Appendix I) The forms outline the terms of engagement, precautions against strikes, together with schedules detailing the different kinds of work and relevant rates of pay. The differences in wages were reflections of the complexity of the task and experience or skill of the operative.

Thus Job Bently, a thrower, was paid 11 and a half pence per score for the wares on his agreed form. His job was to shape and place the clay in the centre of the wheel, then by pressure of his hands and tools, form it into the desired shape. Working on piece rate, the potter would 'throw' all day, pieces of identical size and shape. Master potters would do this with ease and efficiency. Mistakes were costly.

Daniel Williams was a turner, a more exacting task, and the rate of pay varied from one shilling and sixpence per score for 'common ware', two shillings and sixpence per score for water ewers, to three shillings and fourpence per score for 'fancy cups'. His work involved finishing the ware after preliminary shaping and drying to 'leather' hardness. This was accomplished by turning the ware on a lathe which rotated; while rotating, the article was brought into contact with tools of various kinds which trimmed the walls to make them thinner. Incised rings or other forms of decoration were accomplished in this way.

Both trades, throwing and turning, were recognised as very skilled but traditionally, according to Spode records, the 'thrower' was usually paid more, his work being the more highly rated of the two.

WILLIAM MORGAN was employed as a 'dip-turner' which involved dipping ware to be glazed by immersing it in a liquid in which glaze particles were suspended. These were either turned on the wheel or the lathe. The pay of two shillings and sixpence per score for 'ribboned ware', rising to five shillings per score for 'fancy patterns' indicates that this was a complex process and not merely dipping the pot into the glaze.

The pottery could further be enhanced by techniques such as 'scalloping'—shaping the rim to resemble a scalloped shell; 'beading'—applying a pattern of continuous small pottery beads; or 'gadrooning'—applying an ornamental border in a continuous pattern of reeding or fluting set at various angles, often seen on jugs and cups.

Morton Nance also mentions other named workers at the Glamorgan, but I have been unable to trace records of their employment namely, John Vaughan, handler, born in Swansea, 1811, who later worked at Llanelli; David Francis, handler, also worked at Llanelli; Thomas Lindell; James Thomas and Henry Parkes. No records survive of the manager whom Nance names as Evan Davies, nor of the assistant manager, Richard Davies, or foreman, William Davies.

The Forms of Agreement are reproduced as Appendix I. Of the completed forms found, dated 1837, each were signed by the partners at that time, (namely Martin Bevan, Thomas Bevan, William Woodward Haynes and Elizabeth Irwin,) and the workmen. The agent for the pottery was William Bryant who witnessed and signed the contracts. The agreements ensured that any defective wares were to be either broken or refired and that deductions were to be made accordingly from the men's wages. Piece work payment was commonplace in the potteries.

The employers were hard task masters but justifiably so as accidents or mistakes meant a financial loss. The workmen were therefore extra careful in their skills, as imperfect pieces meant loss of wages. The penalties for carelessness were high. L. W. Dillwyn records in his diary of January 1827:

> Drove to Swansea and George Green [Head Gloss Fireman at the Cambrian] was convicted and adjudged to 3 months hard labour in the House of Correction, for having broken or employed others to break, and conceal, large quantities of our ware, which had become damaged through his neglect or carelessness, in order to save himself from being made to pay for the damage.

Identifying the persons responsible for faulty ware was made possible by means of 'Tally Marks'. These were pressers' marks, transferers' marks or painters' marks, which enabled batches of finished pottery or the products of different workmen to be identified. It was important to know whose work was whose, as imperfections or accidental firings could result in serious loss of earnings, and had to be accounted for.

It was commonplace for whole families to be employed at one and the same time in the pottery. The Swansea 1841 census often records fathers with sons and daughters as young as eight or nine residing in Pottery Lane or adjoining streets and noted as a 'potter', or 'working in pottery'. Child labour was cheap—their menial tasks included beating out the clay to get rid of air bubbles before the clay was 'thrown' (otherwise its expansion during firing would spoil the article) or sometimes treading the turner's lathe with their foot, keeping up the speed required in order that the attention of the turner was not distracted from the exacting work on the vessel on which he was working. Generally, children were there to assist the potters, tuners and dippers. Wages were as low as three shillings and sixpence, for a six-day week, working often nine hours a day. Women were traditionally employed as transferers or paintresses, their wages averaging seven to nine shillings per week.

Working conditions within the pottery were both hazardous and dangerous. Many of the raw materials in use in the early 19th century pottery industry later proved to be contributory factors leading to serious health problems and disabilities, some having even fatal consequences.

A glance at the lists of materials in common use will indicate the dangers: Red Lead, Crude Antimony, Litharge (Yellow lead oxide), Copper, Zinc oxide, Dichromate of Potash, Barytes (Barium sulphate). All were potentially dangerous and equally poisonous. Before the dangers of lead poison were fully realised, it was introduced into glazes as a raw lead compound (Red Lead or Lead oxide). Its action in the body was cumulative. Lethargy, drowsiness, muscle and joint pains, anaemia and loss of weight were the usual symptoms, its toxicity building up in the tissues until its presence could no longer be tolerated. Death resulted.

Although lead was always a major hazard for the potter, pneumoconiosis, or 'Potter's Rot', as a result of the inhalation of dust and poisonous fumes, was also a disabling disease in the potteries. It was not confined to one class of worker, but was contracted wherever a workman came into contact with dust. The commonest instances of this were in the handling of powdered flint which produced clouds of fine silica dust. The disease acted gradually and imperceptibly, but with grave consequences. Coupled with incurable infectious diseases like cholera and typhoid, it was little wonder that life expectancy amongst its workers was barely more than forty years. (The average age of death of any skilled manual worker at the time was 37, and little more if you were gentry).

Note 1: The book formed part of a collection of papers relating to Canon Jonn Powell Jones who was born at Gorseinon and later became Rector of Lloughor between 1850-65. The book evidently came into his possession from a family member or parishioner working at The Llanelly Pottery which was distanced only a mile or so from his home at Lloughor.

Chapter 5
SITE EXAVATIONS

During 1983, preparatory excavation work was carried out in the Strand, Swansea, for the construction of a new multi-storey car park to serve Swansea's High Street Railway Station. The 'diggings' led to the discovery of an underground chamber, which was later identified as a drying chamber belonging to the Glamorgan Pottery.

Excavations were carried out in Swansea by the Glamorgan-Gwent Archaeological Trust, who later published an illustrated paper on their findings (*Bulletin of Welsh Medieval Pottery Research Group No.6, 1983,* by S. Sell.)

The construction of the chamber was of a single wall of well rendered stonework with a little brick, and measured 16 by 4 metres. Along its north east-side, a series of four ducts and two tunnels led off at right angles. Within it was a platform built of industrial bricks, which may have been the heating device, with a fire box at one end, and a hot air duct running along its length. Also within the chamber was a series of holes along the walls for supporting timber, racking or shelving. A ground floor room was situated above the drying chamber which was approached by steps above the external cobblestones.

A tunnel led from the underground drying chamber to exit at ground floor level inside an adjacent building, presumably the workshop, where 'throwing' took place. Pots could therefore be transported under cover from the potting room to the underground chamber to dry in a carefully controlled environment.

Much of the internal cavity had been filled in with loose coal 'slack', but excitingly, large quantities of kiln furniture, including saggars, stilts and spurs, (see footnote[1] and Fig. 1) together with fragments of pottery, were discovered. Much of the pottery was plain, cream-coloured ware or whiteware, both in the biscuit, (unglazed) and glazed forms, but some transfer decorated fragments were found. Shards of plates, cups, bowls, tankards and other miscellaneous shapes were noted. Identification of the pottery as being products of

15

Fig. 1

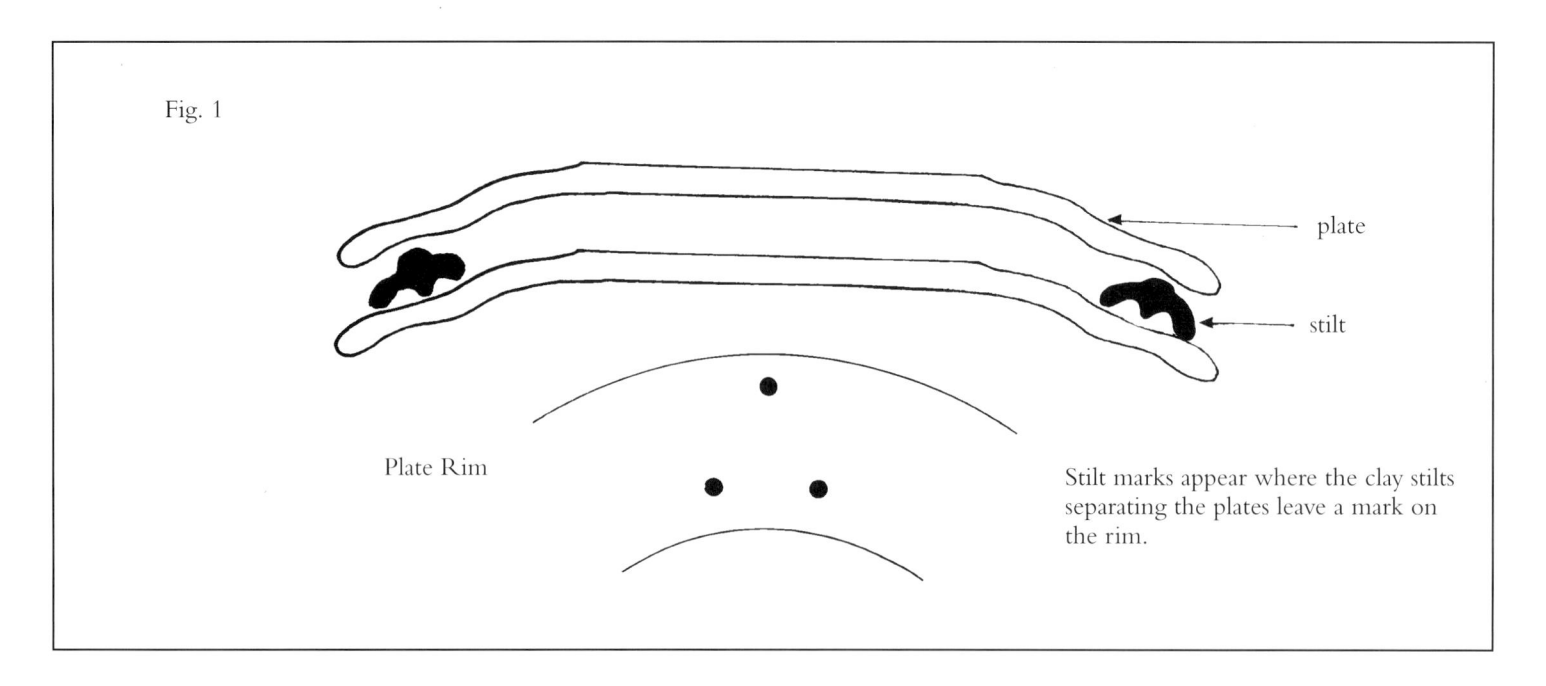

Plate Rim — plate — stilt

Stilt marks appear where the clay stilts separating the plates leave a mark on the rim.

the Glamorgan was provided by impressed stamps bearing the name of Baker, Bevans and Irwin, with and without the impressed Prince of Wales Feathers mark. Pressers' stamps, eight-pointed stars and impressed numbers were also found. The collection of shards recovered were examined and later documented by the late Stanley Williams, a fellow collector and friend, who published his findings in a paper entitled: 'Shards from the Cambrian and Glamorgan Potteries at Swansea', 1986 in *Bulletin of the Welsh Medieval Pottery Research Group, No. 9, 1986-7*.

Tragically, many of the important pieces, notably those inscribed with factory marks, were lost in an extensive fire which broke out at the offices of the Glamorgan-Gwent in Swansea, as a result of which, all the material recovered suffered some damage.

Of the pottery recorded, the following transfer printed patterns were found, both glazed and unglazed:

Ladies of Llangollen,
Pulteney Bridge, Bath,
Willow,
Broseley,
feathered-edge white ware (two rim variations),
glazed creamware,
earthenware 'banded' in black, brown and blue,
'mocha' and 'marbled' ware fragments, in biscuit and glazed forms.

Kiln furniture, including 3-pointed spurs, stilts of various sizes for supporting the pottery during firing, were also collected. Crucibles, conical and 'pinched', which Stanley Williams describes as '3-sided', were recovered in unglazed forms, these presumably being used for the mixing of pigments and enamel colours.

Fortunately, Stanley Williams retained some of the more important fragments excavated as part of his own private collection. When he died in 1989 his extensive collection of Welsh pottery was auctioned where I was fortunate enough to purchase all of his shards, excavated from both the Cambrian and Glamorgan pottery sites in 1983.

Note 1: 'Saggars', or containers of clay, were used to contain the pottery whilst it was being fired. Wares were stacked carefully in the saggars at all stages of firing, to prevent the objects sticking together. Similarly, in order to prevent individual flat items from touching one another during firing, they were stacked horizontally, face down, and separated by 3 'stilts' or 'spurs', resting on the back of the plate below. This was the commonest method of firing, and left 3 single marks on the face of the plates, with three 3-pointed marks on the back of all but the top plate in each pile.

Chapter 6
THE WARES

There is no evidence to suggest that porcelain was ever made at the Glamorgan Pottery, apart from William Weston Young's abortive attempts in 1832. Although Haynes had experimented with a soft paste porcelain using soaprock in his early days at the Cambrian, once at the Glamorgan, he obviously saw no point in financing experiments in which the profits were speculative. He had been witness to many disappointments and failures within the Cambrian, and his years of experience only served to insure his new business against failure. His trade connections were extensive and his excellent grounding in all the tasks involved in pottery manufacture enabled him to supervise the organisation of the new works, and its eventual opening, with confidence.

The products of the Glamorgan were therefore earthenwares, which were primarily of an excellent quality and surprisingly diverse. Several of the Glamorgan patterns are identical to those of the Cambrian. It is very likely that in the earlier days, when the potteries were obvious rivals, a commercially successful pattern or design produced at either pottery would be copied by the opposing factory. The lack of an effective form of protection or copyright before the year 1839 led to patterns often being 'pirated' quite shamelessly by a rival. It has become very difficult to establish which of the two potteries in Swansea in fact originated a pattern which was common to both, e.g. 'The Ladies of Llangollen' or 'Castle Gatehouse', as the copper plate engravings are identical in detail.

However, I am of the opinion that in most cases, if not all, it was the Cambrian who did the copying and not, as has always been assumed, the opposite. When Dillwyn bought the Glamorgan pottery in 1839, the copper plates would have been useful to continue the production of saleable patterns that could have been sold locally. Some matching services may have been required and certainly some existing copper plates would have been used rather than discarded. It must also be remembered that in 1817 Dillwyn relinquished his shares in the Cambrian and sub-let the lease to the new firm of T. & J. Bevington and Co., of which George Haynes senior and George Haynes junior held 3/10ths shares. For a few years, therefore, (1817-21) although Haynes took no active renewed interest in the Cambrian, he would doubtless have been in a position to interchange copper plates between the two potteries.

Table services and tea wares were the chief products, the most popular shapes being jugs, plates, bowls, cups and saucers, mugs, teapots and cow creamers. Toilet wares and commemorative Reform jugs are also fairly widespread. Many interesting shapes are recorded as having been in regular production according to Bryant's notebook, but sadly I have, as yet, been unable to trace them. Printed patterns were popularly received—the black transferred rural scenes, depicting men fishing etc., were produced in large numbers in the 1830-1838 period on moulded jugs in particular, and on the appealing cow creamers, which are often associated with the pottery. With these wares, potters opened up fashionable designs to less wealthy customers. Such staple products offered a quick and assured return.

The wares described in this chapter have been divided into four groups.

Firstly, cream coloured earthenwares: these were the earliest products of the Glamorgan pottery. During the early nineteenth century, a preference grew for a whiter bodied pottery, and creamware lost its popularity.

Secondly, earthenwares painted by freehand. These were produced primarily for ornamentation rather than practical use. The Glamorgan preference for green, red and yellow is very marked, with a predominance of chocolate brown, particularly on the edging of plates.

Thirdly, and by far the largest group in number of designs and variety of shapes, are those wares which were transfer printed. The general high quality of these products was due to an excellence of the printing technique on a fine bodied earthenware. The art of engraving now perfected, the fine Glamorgan printing is seen at its best on the early prints such as the 'Stylised Floral', 'Shepherd' and 'Cowherd' patterns. Almost seventy Glamorgan printed patterns are illustrated, many previously unrecorded, as are newly discovered shapes. The printing is primarily in underglaze blue, but in the 1820's the recently introduced green, brown, black, pink and purple were also used.

The fourth group covers those miscellaneous wares which do not fall into any of the other groups; 'green glazed,' 'sprigged', 'mocha' and 'banded' wares.

GROUP I

CREAMWARE

The body of creamware had been widely used by many other potteries, including the Cambrian, from the late 18th to the beginning of the 19th century. It consisted of ball clay mixed with ground flint, the proportions varying from pottery to pottery. The body was then glazed with a mixture containing lead.

Light in weight, pale cream in colour, the ware is pleasant to handle and use, the glaze soft and often showing an oily irridescence or rainbow effect when held at an angle to the light.

By the time the Glamorgan Pottery had opened in 1814, creamware was becoming unfashionable. Pearlware or plain white bodied wares that could be more easily decorated were now preferred for dinner and dessert wares.

Glamorgan creamware is rare. The majority of pieces seem to have been made for utility, domestic use and left undecorated. Although numerous shards of creamware were excavated on the Glamorgan site, (see Chapter 5) few pieces remain intact.

Of the ceramics collection bequeathed by Colonel Llewellyn Morgan to the Royal Institution in Swansea (now Swansea Museum) in 1927, only one item of Glamorgan creamware is recorded (the majority of pieces bearing the Cambrian Swansea mark and not Glamorgan, as Nance implies). This is the ewer, shown in Plate 1.

PLATE 1 A large, plain creamware ewer, the soft glaze tinged with blue where it lies thickly.
SIZE Ht. 9½ ins.
MARK Impressed 'Baker, Bevans and Irwin' in a horseshoe enclosing a (5).
Swansea Museum, Swansea City Council.

PLATE 2 Creamware platter, painted in sepia.
SIZE 21¼ ins by 16¾ ins.
MARK Impressed 'Baker, Bevans and Irwin' in a horseshoe enclosing (20).
Private Collection.

Of decorated creamware, I know of only two pieces which are identical in size and palette, obviously from the same commissioned service. The delicate painting is in sepia, with an oriental inspired decoration of a Chinese landscape bordered by a series of interlinked diamonds. In the centre is a large chrysanthemum with a smaller spray to the right, both of which emerge from a rocky outgrowth. To the left, a bird sits on the branch of a Lotus Blossom branch which grows out of another rock. The painting is not outstanding but it is competently executed, the sepia decoration complemented well by the plainness of the creamware. It is very reminiscent of Thomas Pardoe's early painting on earthenware at the Cambrian pottery and his later stylised landscapes on Nantgarw porcelain. Although Pardoe had left Swansea by 1810, he may well have taken on commissioned work, possibly as a favour to his old manager, Haynes, or purely in his capacity as a freelance painter.

Also recorded is a chair pan or bidet, housed in a mahogany stand with cover. It had no drainage hole or plug and was impressed 'Baker, Bevans and Irwin' in a horseshoe.

GROUP II

HAND PAINTED WARES

Enamel painting on earthenwares was not practised in any quantity at the Glamorgan Pottery, with the exception of their pierced edge wicker-border plates and previously described unique creamware service.

ARCADED PLATES

These are pierced along the rim, usually in the form of a series of rounded arches, 40 piercings in all. Additional moulding in the form of a basketweave border occurs, usually painted in green but occasionally in red. The central painting is decorated with a group of flowers, sometimes a pink, full blown rose with trailing strawberries or, less commonly, a more delicately painted floral group of flowers in blues, red and green. The rim of the plates is usually painted in a characteristic chocolate brown, sometimes with overpainting on the arches. Similar plates, but of a different mould, were also produced at the Cambrian.

PLATE 3 Plate.
SIZE Diameter 7½ ins.
MARK Impressed 'Baker, Bevans and Irwin' in a horseshoe.
Private collection.

JUGS

The characteristic moulded jugs, made in profusion, I have called the 'Glamorgan' shape (this mould was later used at The Llanelly Pottery and is referred to by this name in *Llanelly Pottery* by G.Hughes and R. Pugh). These are occasionally found with floral enamel painting of a similar palette to the arcaded plates.

Llanelly jugs of this shape have a much bolder decoration of bright blues, orange and green.

At the National Museum of Wales in Cardiff, is a jug with exceptionally fine painting and gilding, attributed to the hand of William Pollard. Born in

PLATE 4 Moulded jug painted by W. Pollard, inscribed, 'J. W. 1829' under the lip in gold.
SIZE Ht. 7¼ ins.
MARK None.
National Museum of Wales, Cardiff.

1803 near Swansea, Pollard was trained as a ceramic painter on porcelain at the Cambrian pottery from the age of about 13-14. His natural artistic ability resulted in his being commissioned to paint the Bevington-Gibbon service at the early age of 17. By 1830, Pollard had moved to King St., Carmarthen where he is recorded as being a 'chinaman' or china dealer. Here he also continued to paint whenever he could on white porcelain or occasionally earthenware, purchased from both the Cambrian and Glamorgan factories. After the death of his wife in May 1833, he returned to Swansea where for many years he earned his livelihood as a china and glass retailer in Castle St—here he used a muffle kiln for firing his own decorated work on pottery and porcelain bought in from other factories. He is regarded as one of the more accomplished flower painters to work at Swansea and was particularly fond of the wild rose, speedwell, auriculas, strawberries and also the passion flower, which seem to have been favourites of his.

PLATE 5 Moulded jug, overpainted in green, blue, pink, orange and brown (pink tending to flake). It is also edged in brown and inscribed on the front (see also Plate 44).
SIZE Ht. 8½ins.
MARK No mark.
Private collection.

PLATE 6 Moulded jug sparsely painted in underglaze blue.
SIZE Ht. 5½ins.
MARK Impressed 'O' and painters dash in underglaze blue.
Swansea Museum, Swansea City Council.

'FEATHER-EDGED' PAINTING

Plain plates and meat platters were sometimes sparsely decorated with an embossed rim, painted under the glaze in blue, known as 'feather-edging'. There are two distinctive moulded borders.

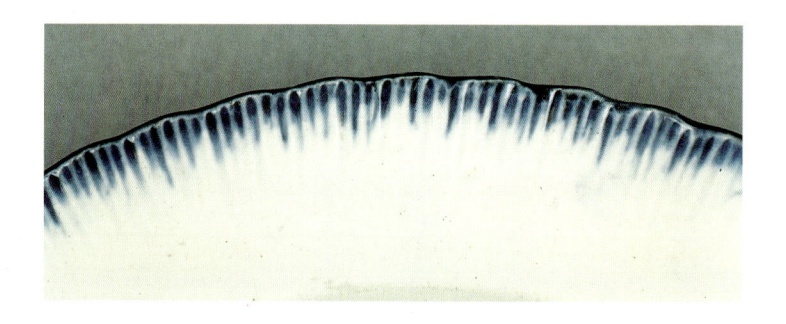

PLATES 7/8 Dinner Plates. SIZE Diameter 7½ins.
MARK Impressed 'Baker, Bevans and Irwin' in a horseshoe.
Swansea Museum, Swansea City Council.

FILLED-IN TRANSFER PRINTED WARES

The technique of painting on top of the underglaze prints to add splashes of colour was an inexpensive method of producing bright colourful pottery with relatively little cost. Less skilled painters and often children would carry out the work well enough to produce a pleasing result. This type of work at the Glamorgan appears to have been well executed and generally by competent hands.

Examples of 'filling-in' of transfers and overpainting of borders is best seen in the wide range of small plates, generally referred to as 'children's plates', although tea wares printed in blue and overpainted in bright colours were also made.

PLATE 9 A part tea service printed in underglaze blue and overpainted in enamel green, orange, yellow, pink and red. It comprises a Teapot, cups and saucers, milk jug, cream jug, slop bowl and, unusually, tea plates. The transfer is of a vase filled with full blown flowers and leaves. Most pieces are marked with the impressed, 'Baker, Bevans and Irwin', in a horseshoe, over 'Swansea', also painters' marks.
Private collection.
A similar pattern was made at the Cambrian Pottery, See Nance Plate XCVI (D).

PLATE 11 A teapot (almost!) with missing handle, spout and lid, but marked with the impressed 'Baker, Bevans and Irwin' mark, in a horseshoe; printed in underglaze blue and overpainted in a similar palette, with an unrecorded pattern. The print shows a chinese lady sitting in a garden seat with elaborate scroll back, an attendant at her side. Private collection.

PLATE 10 Miniature plate, plain rim, printed in underglaze blue and overpainted in enamel colours.
SIZE Diam. 5¾ ins.
MARK Impressed, 'Baker, Bevans & Irwin' in a horseshoe over Swansea enclosing Prince of Wales feathers. Private collection.

FILLED IN TRANSFERS ON MINIATURE PLATES

Small plates with moulded borders, although usually referred to as 'children's plates', vary so much in design and theme, that it is doubtful that their production was intended for children alone—their use was probably purely ornamental and aimed at a much wider market.

The plates in addition to having their transfers filled in with a colourful wash, always had their borders overpainted in bright enamel colours.

As pottery manufacturers could exchange or buy copper plates from one another, and not forgetting that copying was endemic to the trade, it is inevitable that some transfers seen on these Glamorgan plates may be found on similar plates from other factories. Unmarked pieces have therefore been attributed on the basis of not only the transfer, but the moulded border, palette and quality of the earthenware.

Two basic moulded borders exist on miniature plates. The first of these described are those with borders depicting animals.

ANIMAL BORDERS

Whilst several pottery manufacturers produced small plates with animal borders, the Glamorgan miniatures have distinct mouldings in a definite sequence of animals. The order begins (clockwise) with a fox chasing a dog, followed by a flowerhead, another fox then faces a cat, followed by a flowerhead, finally a man

PLATE 12 Blue transfer print of flowers and foliage, overpainted in enamels.
SIZE Diam. 4½ ins.
MARK Baker, Bevans and Irwin over Swansea impressed in a horseshoe around Prince of Wales Feathers.
National Museum of Wales, Cardiff.

PLATE 13 Black transfer print of bird feeding chicks in nest, overpainted in enamel colours.
SIZE Diam. 4½ ins.
MARK Baker, Bevans and Irwin impressed in a horseshoe around a 2, also, 3 printed in blue.
National Museum of Wales, Cardiff.

PLATE 14 Black transfer print of girl and boy with nest full of eggs, overpainted in enamel colours.
SIZE Diam. 4⅞ ins.
MARK Baker, Bevans and Irwin over Swansea impressed in a horseshoe around Prince of Wales Feathers.
National Museum of Wales, Cardiff.

holding a stick and hoop is training a monkey which he holds with a rope, followed by another flowerhead. The flowers are painted in yellow, the animals in browns or rust red.

Several other prints occurs with this border, 'A bird sitting on a basket of fruit', see Nance Pl. XCVI; A mother and children, with verse 'How doth the little busy bee…' (Pl. 23); N. Riley (*Gifts for Good Children*) illustrates a miniature plate of identical form and palette with the inscription, 'Fear God / Honour the / King', which I feel is probably of Glamorgan origin.

THE ROSE AND HONEYSUCKLE BORDER

The border is of alternating Roses and Honeysuckle with leafy sprays connected by swags and garlands. The Honeysuckle is usually painted in a bright yellow, the rose in a rust red, the latter characteristic colour often used as an edging colour. The centres are enamelled in green, brown, yellow and red.

PLATE 15 Black transfer print of a bouquet of flowers and leaves, overpainted in enamel colours.
SIZE Diam. 4⅞ ins.
MARK Baker, Bevans and Irwin over Swansea, impressed in a horseshoe around Prince of Wales Feathers.
National Museum of Wales, Cardiff.

PLATE 16 Blue transfer print of a boy and girl approaching a birds nest, ovepainted in enamel colours.
SIZE Diam. 4⅞ ins.
MARK Baker, Bevans and Irwin, over Swansea, impressed in a horseshoe, around the Prince of Wales Feathers. National Museum of Wales, Cardiff.

PLATE 18 Black transfer print of two vases filled with flowers, overpainted in enamel colours. SIZE Diam. 5 ins.
MARK Baker, Bevans and Irwin impressed, also 3 impressed.
Swansea Museum, Swansea City Council.

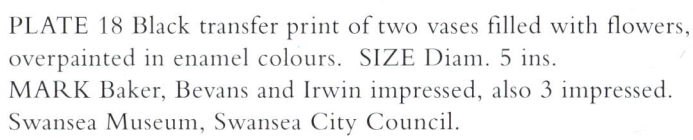

PLATE 17 Black transfer print of a bird feeding chicks in a nest, overpainted in enamel colours.
SIZE Diam. 5 ins.
MARK Baker, Bevans and Irwin in a horseshoe impressed, also 4 impressed, 2 in underglaze blue and painters dash.
Swansea Museum, Swansea City Council.

PLATE 19 Blue transfer print with verse 'MY HEART / IS FIX,D / I CANNOT RANGE / I LIKE MY CHOICE / TOO WELL / TO CHANGE.' and overpainted in enamel colours.
SIZE Diam. 6⅛ ins.
MARK Unmarked. Painters mark in black.
National Museum of Wales, Cardiff.

PLATE 20 Printed in black and enamelled. Print shows a boy leading a pony on which his sister is riding. Inscribed, 'Who taught his Sisters first to ride / Who did the little Poney guide / And with them every Gift divide / My Son.' (From the poem, 'My Son' by Richard Gregory, pub.d. 1812).
SIZE Diam. 4⅞ ins.
MARK Baker, Bevans and Irwin over Swansea impressed in a horseshoe around Prince of Wales Feathers, also painters 2 in brown.
National Museum of Wales, Cardiff.

PLATE 21 Printed in black and enamelled. Print shows baby in a cradle, young boy, young man, and older man, inscribed 'Infancy / Youth / Manhood / and Old Age.'
SIZE Diam. 5 ins.
MARK Baker, Bevans and Irwin impressed in a horseshoe around 4; painters 3 in brown, and 'G' in black.
National Museum of Wales, Cardiff.

PLATE 22 Printed in black and enamelled. Print shows children playing with a Hobby Horse.
SIZE Diam. 4⅞ ins.
MARK Baker, Bevans and Irwin over Swansea impressed in a horseshoe around Prince of Wales Feathers
National Museum of Wales, Cardiff.

PLATE 23 Printed in black and enamelled. Print shows mother and children looking at bee hive, inscribed 'How doth the little busy bee / Improve each shining hour / And gather honey all the day / From every opening flower.'
SIZE Diam. 4⅞ ins.
MARK Baker, Bevans and Irwin in a horseshoe impressed. Painters mark in brown.
Glyn Vivian Art Gallery, Swansea City Council.

PLATE 24 Printed in blue and enamelled. A chinoiserie scene with figures, vase and foliage.
SIZE Diam 6 ins.
MARK Impressed 6 pointed star.
Private collection.

PLATE 25 Printed in black and enamelled. An angel carries a banner inscribed 'AND THE RIGHTEOUS / SHALL BE HAD / IN EVERLASTING / REMEMBRANCE.'
SIZE Diam. 6 ins.
MARK Impressed 8–pointed daisy.
Private collection.

PLATE 26 Printed in black and enamelled. Print of John Wesley in the centre, flanked by figures of Hope and Charity. Inscription reads, 'JEHOVAH reigns let Saints let Men adore / THE REVEREND / JOHN WESLEY M.A.'
SIZE Diam. 6¼ ins. MARK No mark.
Private collection.

PLATE 27 Printed in black and enamelled. Print of ruined Temple.
SIZE Diam. 7 ins.
MARK No mark.
Private collection.

PLATE 28 Printed in black and enamelled. A tree on the left with Abbey ruins.
SIZE Diam. 7 ins.
MARK Painters dash in black.
Private collection.

PLATE 29 Printed in blue and enamelled. Woman with cross beside tomb, inscribed 'There is Rest in Heaven'.
SIZE Diam. 5⅜ ins.
MARK Impressed Diamond.
Private collection.

PLATE 30 Printed in black and enamelled. Nativity scene with Mary and Jesus and inscribed, 'Where is He that is born King of the Jews / For we have seen his star in the East'.
SIZE Diam. 6⅛ ins.
MARK Impressed ▯▯.
Painters mark ✳ in black.
Private collection.

PLATE 31 Printed in black and enamelled. Two women and child seated in garden, inscribed 'PRESENT FOR MY DEAR GIRL.'
SIZE Diam. 6⅛ ins.
MARK Impressed 8 pointed star.
Private collection.

25

I believe it is safe to assume that as no other factory mark has been found on plates with this distinctive border and palette, the following patterns recorded and illustrated in *Gifts for Good Children*, by N. Riley, although unmarked, can safely be ascribed to the Glamorgan pottery. The plate references refer to illustrations in her publication (1991).

CXXV Mrs. Fitzherbert & George IV riding a Hobby Horse, inscribed, 'A vist to Carlton House'. (Impressed H)
CXXXII Venus in her chariot.
CXXXIII Group of children inscribed, 'The Happy Party'.
Pl 249 Female archer with shepherd and sheep.
Pl 948 'Faith'.
Pl 949 'Hope'.
Pl 950 'Charity'.
Pl 951 'Faith Hope and Charity'.
Pl 568 'The Washerwoman'.
Pl 618 Pottery seller with Dutch inscription, 'Eengelsh Steetug'.
Pl 881 Bird amongst flowers.
Pl 889 Chinoiserie group of ladies.
Pl 939 Inscription, 'O may I from sin depart / Have a wise and understanding heart / Jesus to me be given / And let me through the spirit know / To glorify my God below'.
Pl 941 Jesus on Cross, inscribed,'Jesus when he had cried again, with a loud voice yielding up the Ghost.'
Pl 942 Inscription illustrating 'St LUKE CHAP. VII. V14 / The widows son raif,d to life'.
Pl 944 Similar print illustrating 'The Miracle of The Five Loaves and 2 Fithes'.
Pl 983 Illustrates 'The REVEREND JOHN WESLEY' in a circle flanked by figures of Hope and Charity and inscribed, 'I Trust in the Lord and I also myself shall come shortly.'
Pl 985 Wesley preaching in church, inscribed, 'WESLEY speaks from Amos Chap. IV.V.12. Prepare to meet thy God'.
Pl 1043 Woman wtih children going to church, inscribed 'SET GOOD EXAMPLES'.

GROUP III

TRANSFER PRINTED WARES

The technical process whereby a pattern is engraved on to a copper plate, then transferred by inked tissue paper to the surfce of biscuit earthenware is known as transfer printing. After printing, the earthenware is 'fixed' by firing in a kiln and later glazed and fixed again. This process had been a well established practice at the Cambrian under Haynes management. The use of cobalt blue had traditionally been the most popular colour employed throughout the pottery industry although other colours had been experimented with.

Unfired cobalt oxide, when mixed with the printing oil, is a dull purple in colour, not easily visible to the transferer. A vegetable dye was often added to ensure that the design was clearly seen through the transferer's tissue. This gave a greyish colour in appearance which can be seen in the photographs of the biscuit printed shards in Plate 102. When fired in a biscuit kiln, the oil and vegetable colouring is burnt off, leaving the cobalt firmly fixed to the biscuit body and ready for glazing. After dipping in the liquid glaze, the ware was then fired again in the gloss kiln.

After 1815, patterns had become more 'English', with rural country scenes depicted, rather than the much used Chinese inspired oriental views. Predominantly blue, but also pink, green, purple and sepia were colours used for tea and dinner services, although collectors tend to associate the black printed country pastimes scenes as being the hallmark of the Glamorgan Pottery, as they were produced in such large numbers during the latter years. Engraving was at its zenith by 1815-20 and showed superb quality.

SIZES

Dimensions given are to the nearest quarter of an inch. Height is given from the base of the piece to the top of the handle in the case of jugs, mugs and cups, or to the top of the finial in the case of teapots and coffee pots.

PATTERN NAMES

Where pattern names are marked on the wares, they are given within quotes, e.g. 'Vine'. Where any other name is given, it has been adopted to draw attention to its most prominent feature. Patterns are listed here alphabetically.

Birds and Flowers
A pattern of birds sitting on scrolls with elaborate floral bouquets. The border is of intertwined ribbon and flowers and under the spout, a secondary transfer has been applied from the Rural scenes series depicting, mother, child and dog. Interestingly, these transfers together with the ribbon border, were also used on the Ship jug, Pl. 88.

PLATE 32 Teapot printed in blue.
SIZE Ht. 6½ ins. Length 10 ins.
MARK 'Opaque China' over 'B. B.) I' in a scroll, printed in blue.
National Museum of Wales, Cardiff.
See also Plate 135 for teapot shape.

Bridge and Tower
The pattern shows two men fishing from a two arched bridge. To the left is a tall tower, to the right, an overhanging tree with gatehouse. A church and trees form the background. Found in brown on tea wares; also a blue printed mug is shown (See Pl. 150).

PLATE 33 Teapot printed in brown.
SIZE Length 10½ ins. Ht. 7 ins. MARK 'Opaque China' over 'B. B. & I' in a scroll, printed in brown, also transferers 4 in brown.

PLATE 34 Milk jug, from the same service.
SIZE Length 5⅞ ins. Ht. 4½ ins.
MARK As above.

Plates 33 and 34 are from a private collection of a complete tea set, comprising 6 cups and saucers, teapot, milk jug and sugar bowl.

Broseley

A chinoiserie design which includes a large pagoda-like temple on the left with a willow tree on the right overhanging a bridge on which two Chinese figures are crossing. On jugs and mugs, the pattern is often printed in reverse. There appear to be minor variations in the transfers, depending on the size of the piece. The figures usually, but not invariably, carry umbrellas. Both variations are found with a factory mark. The pattern has a distinct moth border, absent on miniature plates. Similar transfers were used by other factories including Davenport, Rogers, Wedgwood and the Cambrian on pottery, also Spode on bone china.

Found in pale blue only on toilet sets, thrown, round jugs, miniature plates, an egg-cup stand.

'Campania'

The pattern shows an oriental figure riding an elephant and carrying a parasol while another figure stands nearby. To his right, is a tall vase on a plinth with a background of foliage. The border is made up of vignettes of alternating pagodas and flowers. Found in green, black and purple on tea wares.

PLATE 35 Miniature plate, printed in blue.
SIZE Diameter 4½ ins.
MARK Printed, 'Opaque china' over 'B. B. & I' in a scroll.
Private collection.

PLATE 36
'Thrown' Round Jug,
printed in blue.
SIZE Ht. 7¼ ins.
MARK No mark.
Private collection.

PLATE 37 Jug with elaborate leaf moulding under spout and scalloped moulding on base and rim, scroll handle with curled floral termination at bottom of handle. Printed in black.(Rare shape.)
SIZE Ht. 7¼ ins.
MARK Impressed 5-pointed star on base of handle.
Private collection.

A teapot in the collection of the National Museum of Wales, Cardiff, printed in this pattern, bears the impressed mark 'Baker, Bevans and Irwin', also an impressed crown and figure 7, in addition to the transferred 'Campania' mark. (For mark, see Plate 174). This pattern was also used at the Cambrian pottery.

Castle Gatehouse

This print is common to both factories at Swansea and is an early design. At the Cambrian, it was certainly in use C 1818, as it is found on porcelain impressed 'Bevington & Co.' in addition to pottery examples. There are no differences in the copper plates. The print is based on an aquatint contained in 'Views of Rome and its vicinity' published by J. Merigot, London, 1769-98. The castle is taken from a view entitled 'The Gate of Sebastian at Capena' and was first introduced by Spode in 1806. The Spode print and the Cambrian are usually very pale blue, whereas the Glamorgan examples are a comparatively deeper blue in colour. Found in blue on dinner wares; plates, tureens, strainers, pickle dishes.

PLATE 38 Tureen Stand.
SIZE Diam. 13 ins.
MARK Printed 'Opaque China' over 'B. B. & I' in an elaborate scroll, also an impressed 6.
Private collection.

Commemorative Wares

The tradition of depicting historical public events on pottery were little practiced at the Glamorgan Pottery, although during its productive years, the following main events took place between the years 1814-1838.

1815 The Battle of Waterloo.
1816 Princess Charlotte married.
1817 Princess Charlotte died.
1820 George III died. Prince Regent became George IV.
1821 George IV crowned. Death of Queen Caroline.
1830 George IV died. William acceded.
1831 William IV and Queen Adelaine crowned.

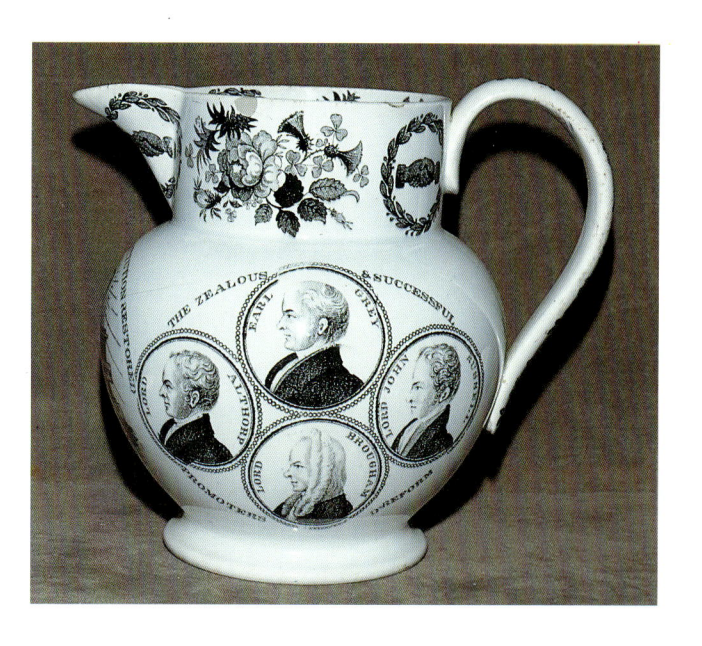

PLATE 39 Thrown jug, printed in black.
SIZE Ht. 6 ins. MARK 'Opaque China' over 'B. B. & I.' in a scroll, printed in black.
Private collection.

Reform Jugs

The most notable of the Glamorgan Pottery commemoratives were the transfer printed 'Reform' jugs. The agitations that culminated in the Great Reform Bill of 1832, resulted in the most prolifically commemorated political event of 19th century British History. Once the Napoleonic wars were over, Parliamentary reform was soon on the minds of the British public - the country suffering greater and greater unrest.

29

PLATE 40 Thrown jug, printed in blue.
SIZE Ht. 6 ins.
MARK 'Opaque China' over 'B. B. & I.' in a scroll, printed in blue.
Glynn Vivian Art Gallery, Swansea City Council.

PLATE 41 Moulded jug, printed in purple.
SIZE 6½ ins.
MARK No mark.
Swansea Museum, Swansea City Council.

In 1830, William IV ascended the throne and on March 1st, 1831, Greys new Government introduced the long awaited Reform Bill. It was not received well by the majority of the House and was frought with problems and repeated opposition over the next year. Undaunted, Lord John Russell produced an amended Bill which was eventually passed in June 1832.

Transfers of the four main heroes of the Bill appear on Glamorgan jugs; LORD ALTHORP, LORD BROUGHAM, EARL GREY and LORD JOHN RUSSELL.

The jugs show four linked circular medallions in which named portraits of the four reformers appear. Linking the medallions are the words 'THE ZEALOUS & SUCCESSFUL PROMOTERS OF REFORM' and on the reverse, 'ROYAL ASSENT / TO THE / REFORM / BILL / 7 JUNE 1832'.

Several variations exist depending on the size of the jug, the smaller jugs having only 2 portraits. The transfers can be found on round, thrown jugs or the moulded, Glamorgan shaped jugs, usually in black, occasionally purple, rarely blue.

O' Connell Jugs
Daniel O'Connell was the founder of the Roman Catholic Association and the prime campaigner for Catholic emancipation, both in Ireland and in Britain.

He was elected member of Parliament for the county of Clare in 1828 and several commemorative jugs were made to celebrate his election, produced primarily for the Irish market.

PLATE 42/43 Thrown jug printed in black.
SIZE Ht. 4¾ ins.
MARK No mark. Private collection.

His victory was depicted on small, rounded thrown jugs and also on Glamorgan shaped jugs with a slight variation in the moulding.

The transfers are always in black, with a portrait of Daniel O'Connell on one side, and Father Matthew, the great advocate of total abstinence or teetotalism, on the other. On the front, the inscription reads:

Dan O Connel Esq.
and
The Very Revd. Father Matthew
The Two Great
Regenerators
of
Ireland.

A wreath of shamrock and rye are printed around the rim. The handle and spout are overpainted in black in the usual way.

Personal Commemoratives

Purely personal events such as births, christenings, marriages etc. are occasionally found commemorated on Glamorgan Pottery. Named and dated pieces could easily be commissioned by visitors to the pottery, as was often the case with the crew of sea going vessels who would have called with regularity in Swansea. Hence, both Welsh and West country names appear. The following are a few examples:

PLATE 44 Moulded Glamorgan shaped jug, hand painted in enamel colours, inscribed in brown 'Willm. Featherstone 1816. Aug.t. 31 st'. SIZE Ht. 8½ ins. MARK No Mark. Private collection.

PLATE 45 Moulded Glamorgan shaped jug, printed in sepia with transfers from the Rural series inscribed 'Mr. Wm. Crang / Wheitefield / Barton / Challacombe / Bought at Swansea / By / Captn. Irwin / 1831'.

The jug is one of a set of three graduated jugs. This is not 'the' Captain Irwin of the pottery, but possibly his son, who might have joined the merchant navy after his father. There was also a family of this name living at Ilfracombe whose memebrs had naval connections.   SIZE 10 ins.
MARK 'Opaque China' over 'B. B. & I.' in a scroll, printed in sepia.   Private collection.

PLATE 46 Moulded Glamorgan shaped jug printed in black with transfers from the Rural series and inscribed in black. 'ELIZABTH HICKs WILLIAMS / BORN DECbr. 20th. 1835' SIZE 6½ ins.   Private collection.

31

CONTINUOUS 'SHEET' PATTERNS

Bells
A bold continuous sheet pattern of bell-like flowers with interlacing stems in a dark flow blue. This teapot is of identical shape to the marked teapot illustrated in Plate 131. I believe this pattern to be of Glamorgan origin, the copper plates used later at the Cambrian Pottery on tea wares (1830s-50s). See M. Nance, Pl. LXXVI (E)

stars. Printed in green with over painting in red. Found on moulded jugs in green, blue and purple.

'Vine'
A continuous pattern of vine leaves and tendrils with bunches of hanging grapes. Found in pink and purple on tea wares and moulded jugs.

PLATE 47 Teapot printed in blue.
SIZE Ht. 7¼ ins. Length 11 ins.
MARK No mark. Private collection.

PLATE 49 Moulded jug printed in purple.
SIZE Ht. 8½ ins.
MARK Special backstamp 'VINE', above 'B. B. & I'. in a scroll and leaf frame, printed in purple. (See Plate 176). Also, an impressed 5. Private collection.

Quilted
A continuous sheet pattern which resembles quilted

'Cottage Girl'
The transfer shows a girl with a dog and two pails of

PLATE 48 Moulded jug printed in green with overpainting.
SIZE Ht. 6¼ ins.
MARK Impressed 3. Private collection.

PLATE 50 Thrown Jug, printed in blue.
SIZE Ht. 7 ins.
MARK Special backstamp 'Cottage Girl' printed in blue in a drape overhanging 'B. B. & I.' (See Plate 175). Private collection.

water at her feet which she has drawn from a nearby stream. The hoop over her shoulder is used to support the pails when carried. A cottage and mountainous landscape form the background.

The design is taken from a painting 'The Cottage Girl' by H. Howard R. A., later engraved by W. Finden, published 1831.

Found in blue on thrown, round jugs; tea-wares.

Cowherd

An unrecorded pattern. The transfer shows a man sitting beneath a tree with 2 cows alongside a river. The cowherd, with stick in hand, is leaning against one of the cows. A castle forms the background.

Found in blue only on a teapot.

Although unmarked, the pottery characteristics and shape, indicate a Glamorgan origin. This pattern is also recorded on a Cambrian teapot of later shape.

PLATE 51 Teapot printed in blue.
SIZE Ht. 6¼ ins. Length 10 ins.
MARK Impressed 15. Private collection.

PLATE 52 Moulded jug, printed in blue. SIZE Ht. 7 ins.
MARK 'Opaque China' over 'B. B. & I.' in a scroll, printed in blue.
Private collection.

on table wares, moulded jugs in blue, sepia, black and green.

An extensive dinner service printed in blue in this pattern is housed at the National Museum of Welsh Life, St. Fagans, Cardiff, and comprises the following:

Large Soup Tureen with cover, Stand and Ladle
3 Soup Plates
Large Meat Platter
5 Vegetable Tureens and covers
7 Dinner Plates
Dish for fish with Strainer
Salad Bowl
Pair of small Sauce Tureens with Stands and Ladles
Large Comport for cheese
3 small Plates for sweets/pickles
2-handled Bowl

Floral

A popular pattern of bouquets and sprays of garden flowers, sometimes with butterflies and insects. Found

'Gothic border'
A previously unrecorded pattern. The print shows a woman and child walking along a road towards a village, with a church in the distance. A large tree overhangs the picture on the right, while a two-handled urn sits on a pedestal on the left. The pattern name refers to the wide gothic border alternating with floral reserves. Only one bowl recorded.

PLATES 53/54 Bowl.
SIZE Ht. 3¼ ins. Diameter 6¾ ins (Top), 3⅜ins (Bottom).
MARK Special backstamp. 'Gothic Border' over 'B. B. & I.' in a scroll (See Plate 171).
Glyn Vivian Art Gallery, Swansea City Council.

'Harper'
The pattern shows a bearded bard, seated on a rocky outcrop, playing a harp. He overlooks a lake with mountainous background. The pattern has a deep scroll and foliate border.

Found in blue on tea wares, particularly slop bowls. A teapot is also recorded, See Plate 127.

PLATE 55 Bowl
SIZE Diam. 6 1/2 ins. Ht. 3 3/8 ins.
MARK Special backstamp 'B. B. & I.' above 'Harper', printed in blue. (See Plate 172). Private collection.

'Haymaker'
Depicts a peasant girl in wide brimmed hat holding a

PLATE 56 Bowl printed in blue.
SIZE Diam 6½ ins. Ht. 3⅜ ins.
MARK Special backstamp 'Haymaker' over 'B. B. & I.' in a scroll, also transferers 2 in blue (See Plate 173). Private collection.

rake standing in a hayfield. Behind her, two men are loading hay on to a cart, in the background, a farmhouse, shed and trees.

Found in blue on tea wares, particularly slop bowls. A teapot is also recorded. See Pl. 131.

The Ladies of Llangollen
Traditionally, this popular pattern is thought to represent Lady Eleanor Butler and Miss Sarah Ponsonby, the daughters of Anglo Irish aristocrats who, when given a small allowance, eloped from Ireland in 1778 and set up home across the waters in North Wales, in the town of Llangollen. They converted and extended their cottage, re-naming it 'Plas Newydd', the New Place. The print shows two ladies on horseback in riding habit, one talking to a man holding a scythe. Two cows drink from a river which flows down past a house with a water mill. An Italianate castle sits on the hillside in the left of the pattern, while to the right, lie houses and a church. The print is obviously not a true representation of the town. The wide border is a design of flower heads and alternating cobweb-like motifs.

This print is also found on Cambrian pottery marked either 'Dillwyn' in a half circle or 'Dillwyn' over 'Swansea' impressed. The quality of the pottery on the Cambrian examples is thicker and heavier in comparison, indicating a post 1830 period. In my opinion, the Glamorgan examples usually have a sharper print and are always a much deeper blue.

Found in blue on dinner wares, thrown rounded jugs.

Mandarin with Chinese Lantern
An oriental inspired pattern surrounded by a wide border of flower heads and delicate leaf sprays. The central pattern shows two oriental figures, the

PLATE 57 Dinner Plate.
SIZE Diameter 10 ins.
MARK Impressed Prince of Wales Feathers Mark.
Private collection.

PLATE 58 Saucer dish.
SIZE Diam. 7¾ ins.
MARK Printed 'Opaque China' over 'B. B. & I.' in a leafy scroll. Also an impressed 6-pointed star.
Swansea Museum, Swansea City Council.

Mandarin carrying a Chinese Lantern with a female figure at his side holding a parasol. A temple and Chinese landscape frame the figures.
    Found in pale blue on tea wares.

Mandarin with pipe
This pattern is enclosed within a central medallion surrounded by a wide rococo border of stylised flower heads and foliage. In the centre are three oriental figures, the seated Mandarin on the right smokes a

> PLATE 59 Saucer, printed in blue.
> SIZE Diam. 5¾ ins.
> MARK Printed 'Opaque China' over 'B. B. & I.' in a leafy branch. This mark occurs only on 'Mandarin' patterns. (See Pl. 170). Private collection.

long stemmed pipe, while to his left a child leans against a chair supported by another figure.
    The pattern is found in pale blue on tea and coffee wares.

Parrot
An unrecorded pattern. The pattern is enclosed within a central medallion surrounded by a wide border of foliage on a delicate background. In the centre, a parrot, which has flown from the open door of a bird cage, is perched on a branch amongst flowers and leaves.
Found in pink on a cup and saucer.

> PLATE 60 Cup and Saucer.
> SIZE Cup, Ht. 2ins, Diam (top) 3¾ ins; Saucer, Diam. 5¾ ins.
> MARK 'Opaque China' over 'B. B. & I.' in a scroll, printed in pink. Transferers 3 in pink. Private collection.
> For shape, see Pl. 149.

Pulteney Bridge, Bath
The print is loosely derived from an engraving by W. Byrne after the watercolour by Thomas Hearne 1792. The Hearne painting is now in the collection of the Yale Center for British Art, New Haven, Connecticut. The engraver for the pottery print has reversed the image so that the church of St. Michaels which should be on the left, is on the right. The church is also shown with a spire which it did not have at the time of the engraving. The three arched bridge over the river Avon was built in 1770 by Sir William Pulteney.
    In the foreground, a man is seated on the river bank with a stick in his right hand, while two bonneted ladies are punted down the river by standing male

figures. The background shows deer grazing in a wooded hillside with two figures walking the hill. The wide border is of Poppy heads and foliage.

This pattern was mistakenly ascribed by P. Pryce and S. Williams ('Swansea Blue and White Pottery' 1972) to the Cambrian pottery based on a puzzle jug of similar Cambrian shape (See Pl. 163/4). Only pieces marked with a Glamorgan factory mark are recorded, while the known puzzle jug depicting this pattern is of a different shape and has a different pierced pattern to those from the Cambrian factory.

Found in blue on toilet sets, thrown round jugs, puzzle jugs.

Rural Series
Perhaps the most characteristic and familiar transfers produced at the Glamorgan are those which depict fishing, garden and country scenes, usually printed in black, sometimes in sepia. In all, over 40 different prints have been recorded in this popular series, some of which are illustrated in this section.

They are typically found on moulded 'Glamorgan' shaped jugs which seem to have been produced in prolific numbers, also, on mugs, miniature plates, cow creamers and tea wares. Sometimes 'Fishing', and 'Garden' prints occur on the same piece, with often, smaller transfers of cottages or chalets appearing inside the rims of jugs or the lids of teapots.

PLATES 61/62 Moulded Water Jug.
SIZE Ht. 9 ins.
Mark Impresed 'Baker, Bevans and Irwin' enclosing 4.
Private collection.

PLATE 63
Miniature plate with floral and scale border, the centre printed in black with country scene of girl feeding ducks on a pond.
SIZE Diam. 6 ins.
MARK 'Opaque China' over 'B. B. & I.', printed in black.
Private collection.

37

PLATES 64/65 Miniature plates with floral and scale moulding around the border, the centres printed in black with fishing scenes.
SIZE Diam. 6 ins.
MARKS 'Opaque China' over 'B. B. & I.', printed in black, also impressed Baker, Bevans and Irwin in a horseshoe, encircling 4. Private collection.

PLATE 66 Miniature plate with painted blue border, the centre printed in black with fishing scene.
SIZE Diam. 6 ins.
MARK 'Opaque China' over 'B. B. & I.', printed in black. Private collection.

PLATE 67 Moulded 'Glamorgan' shaped jug printed in black with two country scenes of Swiss chalets and girl herding goats.
MARK 'Opaque China' over 'B. B. & I.', printed in black. Swansea Museum, Swansea City Council.

PLATE 68 Cream jugs printed in black with Fishing scenes.
MARKS 'Opaque China' over 'B. B. & I.', printed in black. Private collection.
(See also Pl. 143 under 'Shapes').

PLATE 69 Teapot with floral mouldings around collar, printed in black with Fishing scenes.
SIZE Ht. 7½ ins. L. 11 ins.
MARK 'Opaque China' over 'B. B. & I.', printed in black.
Swansea Museum, Swansea City Council.
(See also Pl. 131 for shape.)

PLATES 70/71 Mug with indented sides and gadrooned rim and base, printed in black with garden scenes, Mother and child with dog; Reverse, girl holding dove.
SIZE Ht. 3 ins. Diam. (top) 3¼ ins.
MARK 'Opaque China' ove 'B. B. & I.', printed in black.
Private collection.

PLATES 72/73 Moulded 'Glamorgan' shaped jug, printed in sepia. Left, Mother holding child on dog's back (inside rim); Gentleman on bench looking at lady with parasol; Fishing scenes. Reverse, repeat pattern of above; child feeding lamb, fishing scene.
SIZE 10 ins.
MARK 'Opaque China' over 'B. B. & I.', printed in sepia.
Private collection.

39

PLATES 74/75 Moulded 'Glamorgan' shaped jug printed in black with four different Fishing scenes. Private collection.

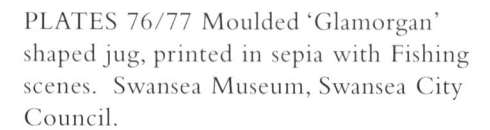

PLATES 76/77 Moulded 'Glamorgan' shaped jug, printed in sepia with Fishing scenes. Swansea Museum, Swansea City Council.

All jugs illustrated in this series are marked with the standard printed 'Opaque China' over 'B. B. & I.' in a scroll.

PLATES 78/79 Moulded 'Glamorgan' shaped jug printed in black. Left, fishing scene; mother picking flowers and child with outstretched arms. Right, fishing scene; mother sitting child on dog's back. Private collection.

PLATES 80/81 Moulded 'Glamorgan' shaped jug printed in black with four different fishing scenes. Private collection.

Shells and flowers
A popular design, used on table wares, 'thistle'-shaped vases, mugs and moulded jugs. Found in blue, sepia, black.

Shepherd
An unrecorded pattern. The transfer shows a shepherd in checkered breeches wearing a large plumed hat. He is leaning on his crook while tending his sheep which are grazing under a tree. In the background are a castle and a cottage. On the reverse of the transfer, another shepherd is sitting under a tree with a girl in a wide brimmed hat. An additional transfer appears on the bowl of a boy with a stick, riding a donkey.

Found only in blue on a coffee pot, bowl and cups.

PLATE 82 Breakfast cup and saucer with gadrooned rim, printed in sepia.
SIZE Cup, Ht. 2½ ins, Diam. (top) 4¾ ins, Saucer, Diam. 6¾ ins.
MARK 'Opaque China' over 'B. B. & I.', printed in brown.
Private collection.

PLATES 83, 84, 85 Cup of French shape, and bowl, printed in blue.
SIZE Cup. Ht. 2¾ ins, Diam. (Top) 3½ ins, Bowl, Diam. 6½ ins, Ht. 3ins.
MARK 'Opaque China' over 'B. B. & I.' in a scroll, printed in blue.
Private collection.

41

Ships

Plates and jugs decorated with ships were manufactured to meet a demand created by the many seamen who frequented the port of Swansea and also those who had close links with the transport of raw materials to and from the South West corner of England. The vessels depicted were sailing brigs of the early nineteenth century and were accurate in many details. Occasionally, a piece will have a name, date or inscription to commemorate a personal event.

PLATE 86 Plate printed in blue
with two masted sailing ship.
SIZE Diam. 10¼ ins.
MARK Impressed 12.
Private collection.

PLATE 87 Plate printed in blue
with three masted sailing ship.
SIZE Diam. 10¼ ins.
MARK Impressed 12.
Private collection.

Two ship designs are known on Glamorgan pottery. The first shows a two masted brig, usually transferred in underglaze black (on jugs) or blue (on plates). The distinctive border shows Britannia, with Neptune sailing the waves in a chariot pulled by sea horses.

The second design is of a three masted sailing ship in full sail. In the foreground of the design, the initials G P Co / S, standing for Glamorgan Pottery Co. Swansea, occur in very small blurred letters on a bale of goods and on the head of a barrel. This method of marking (in addition to the backstamp) is unique. The border accompanying these ships is usually that of the first desgin (nautical emblems) but a jug in the National Museum of Wales, Cardiff, shows a completely different border (See Plate 88) of intertwined ribbon and floral sprays. Secondary transfers of the 'bird and flowers' design have been applied to the neck, and a design from the 'Rural Scenes' under the handle of the jug.

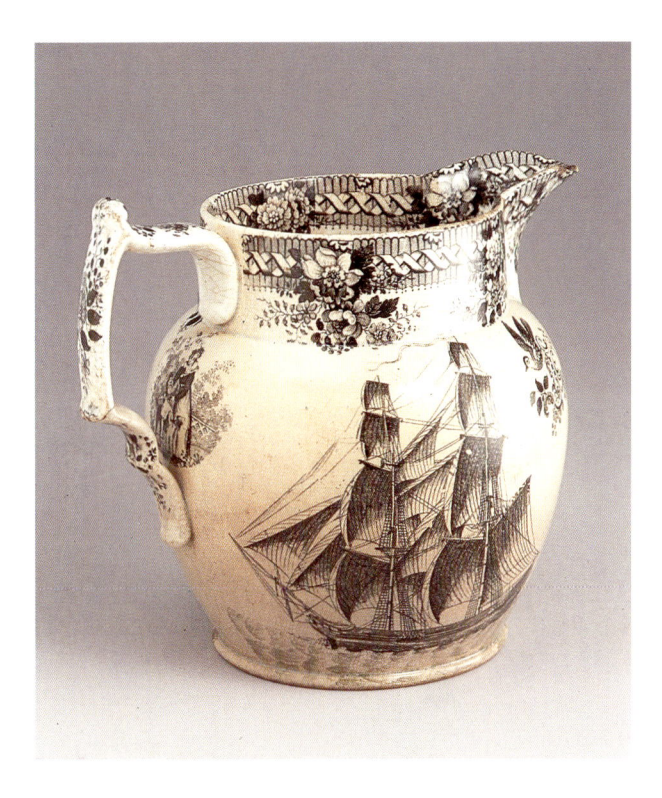

PLATE 88 Thrown jug, printed in black and green, with two masted sailing ship, ribbon border and small transfer from Rural series under spout.
SIZE Ht. 7 ins.
MARK 'Opaque China' printed in blue over 'B. B.& I.' in a scroll.
National Museum of Wales, Cardiff.

PLATE 89 Thrown jug printed in black, with two masted sailing ship and nautical emblem border. Overpainted floral sprays in red and green and inscribed in black, 'Ed. Jones'. Handle not original.
SIZE Ht. 7 ins.
MARK 'Opaque China' printed in black over 'B. B. & I.' in a scroll. Transferers 3.
Swansea Museum, Swansea City Council.

Stylised Floral
This is one of the earliest Glamorgan transfers and is very reminiscent of prints used by 18th. century English porcelain factories such as Worcester, Caughley and Liverpool etc. It is usually found on lightly potted pearlware of exceptional quality, in blue only.

PLATE 90 Plain edged dinner plate, printed in blue.
SIZE Diam. 9 ins.
MARK Impressed Baker, Bevans and Irwin in a horseshoe over Swansea, also impressed 'H'.
Private collection.

'Tower'
This pattern depicts a castellated tower to the left of the print with two women and a child standing in a roadway leading to a church. To the right is a Monopteros or circular temple of pillars supporting a roof. In the distance is a mountainous background. The wide border is of foliage and scroll work.

43

PLATE 91 Moulded Water Jug, printed in blue.
SIZE Ht. 9½ ins.
MARK Impressed 'O'. Private collection

Usually found in blue or black on toilet wares and occasionally dinner wares.

Willow
This popular pattern was produced throughout the working life of the pottery, mainly for dinner wares. Found in blue only.

Plates 93/94.
Enlargement of plate to show S mark.

Unusually, many Glamorgan 'Willow' patterned plates have a factory mark incorporated into the copper plate engraving. A capital 'S' for Swansea appears clearly within a box or window alongside the tree on the extreme right of the print. This mark, together with the G. P. Co/S mark found on ship plates, is rare in that both occur on the *front* of the design.

PLATE 92 Dinner Plate with plain rim.
SIZE 10 ins.
MARK Impressed H also impressed Baker, Bevans and Irwin in a horseshoe over Swansea. Private collection.

GROUP IV

MISCELLANEOUS WARES

GREEN GLAZED WARES

Green glazes on pottery had been perfected by Josiah Wedgwood as early as 1760. The recipe for the glaze contained flint, glass, red lead, white enamel and vitrified, calcined copper. Swansea, together with other potteries, copied these attractive wares. Those of the Glamorgan have quite distinctive shapes. Dishes and plates modelled in the form of leaves, embossed with veins, some representing vine leaves, others with superimposed leaves are known. It must be remembered that under Haynes's management considerable amounts of green glazed pottery had been successfully marketed at the Cambrian pottery years before. (See G. Davidson's article on 'The early Pottery of Swansea', 1968).

PLATE 96 Green glazed dish.
SIZE Length 10¾ ins.
MARK No mark. Private collection.

PLATE 97 Green glazed dish.
SIZE Length 10½ ins.
MARK 'Baker, Bevans and Irwin' impressed in a horseshoe, enclosing 2. Private collection.

PLATE 95 An oval pierced edge dish, the base of a chestnut basket. The dish is beautifully modelled, thinly potted and shows a bright, irridescent glaze as do all of the green glazed wares. The irregularity of the circular border pattern shows evidence of being cut by hand.
SIZE Length 10½ ins.
MARK Impressed 'Baker, Bevans and Irwin' in a horseshoe. Private collection.

PLATE 98 Green glazed plate.
SIZE Diameter 8½ ins.
MARK Impressed 8-pointed daisy (See Pl. 177). Swansea Museum, Swansea City Council.

45

'SPRIGGED' WARES

'Sprigging' was a technical process which involved the application of a decorative motif made in a separate mould to the main body of the clay. At the Glamorgan, jugs were made in this way.

PLATE 99
Sprigged jug.
SIZE Ht. 9 ins.
MARK Impressed 'Baker Bevans and Irwin' in a horseshoe.
Swansea Museum, Swansea City Council.

PLATE 100
Sprigged jug.
SIZE Ht. 6 ins.
MARK Impressed 'Baker Bevans and Irwin' in a horseshoe, enclosing 7.
Private collection.

'Sprigged' jugs

These are moulded, octagonal jugs with sprigs of applied flower stalks, acanthus leaves and sprays of flower heads. The designs were those which resembled similar jugs being modelled at Wedgwods factory at this time. The sprig mould was filled with coloured clay, and applied to the body of the jug before firing. The potter would take pains to finish neatly the sprig motifs and then apply them deftly to the jugs. The glaze was applied thinly to avoid obscuring the details. There are two variations in the types of sprigging which occur usually in a pale blue but occasionally in a rust red. Sizes vary from 6 ins to 10¼ ins and the arrangement of the sprigging may also vary.

PLATE 101 Sprigged jug. SIZE Ht. 10¼ ins.
MARK Impressed 'Baker Bevans and Irwin' in a horseshoe, enclosing 5. Swansea Museum, Swansea City Council.

'MOCHA', 'BANDED' and 'MARBLED' WARE

'MOCHA' ware is known to have been made at both the Glamorgan and the Cambrian potteries as large numbers of biscuit and glazed shards have been excavated from both sites. This type of ware was being made throughout the pottery industry in the early 19th century, although many specimens are impossible to date and rarely bear factory marks.

On to a broad band of coloured slip, usually cream, blue, yellow or a pale turquoise, the 'mocha' decoration was applied. The potter would use a contrasting pigment, black or brown, mixed with a 'tea', said to consist of tobacco juice, Tansy leaves or urine, (each potter would have his own particular recipe) and apply this to the pot. While the band of slip was still wet, the 'tea' was blown on, and the resultant 'fanning out' formed a decoration which resembled trees, seaweed, moss or ferns.

Mugs and jugs for public houses were decorated in this way and after the 1820's, bear an 'excise mark' applied by the weights and measures office. The marks when they contain numbers, indicate the town or district in which the pots were tested and marked - they verified the true liquid capacity according to an official procedure of measurement.

The official Excise Stamp numbers for Glamorgan are 280, 282, 284-289 and for Swansea 295.

'BANDED' ornamentation was made by applying different colours of slip in concentric rings around the vessel, usually jugs and mugs. Sometimes the bands were cut through the slip on the lathe, to produce a pattern with the underlying body. On excavated glazed shards, colours found were, brown and orange bands on a cream ground; blue and black bands on a white ground and blue and black bands on a cinnamon ground.

Biscuit shards of earthenware decorated with a 'MARBLED' effect were also excavated from the site, proof that this technique was employed at the Glamorgan. Of the glazed shards found, the marbling is in blues, browns and cream colours.

Plate 102 Examples of biscuit and glazed shards excavated from the Glamorgan pottery site.

SHAPES

William Bryant's note book gives us some idea of the range of shapes that were thrown or turned at the pottery and in everyday use in the year 1838. The shapes probably reflect the way of life of the middle classes rather than the working class family, as decorated pottery was a luxury affordable only by the privileged few of some means. A record of the moulded pottery shapes can only be built up from surviving examples. Unfortunately, many of the items listed in Bryant's workbook still remain a mystery, but it is hoped that in time, some of them may come to light.

'Gadrooning' which was a characteristic feature on many Glamorgan shapes, was generally introduced in the ceramic industry in the early 1820's.

The wares have been divided here into 5 groups:
    Dinner wares
    Jugs
    Breakfast and Tea wares
    Toilet wares
    Decorative or Ornamental wares.

PLATE 103 Indented platter, printed in blue with Castle Gatehouse pattern.
SIZE L. 12½ ins. W. 16½ ins.
MARK 'Opaque China' over 'B. B. & I.' in a scroll, printed in blue.
Private collection.

DINNER WARES

Dinner being the main meal of the day and often comprising several courses, followed by a sweet or dessert, lent itself to a variety of different shapes and sizes in plates and serving dishes.

PLATE 104 Indented platter, printed in blue with floral transfers.
SIZE L. 22 ins. W. 17¾ ins.
MARK 'Opaque China' over 'B. B. & I.' in a scroll.
Impressed 20.
Swansea Museum, Swansea City Council.

PLATE 105 Salad/Fruit Bowl, printed in blue with Floral pattern.
SIZE Diam. 9½ ins.
MARK 'Opaque China' printed over 'B. B. & I.' in a scroll.
Swansea Museum, Swansea City Council.

PLATE 106 Group of Dinner wares, printed in blue with Floral pattern.
SIZES Tureen L. 12¼ ins. W. 8⅝ ins.
Ladle L. 7½ ins. Diam of bowl, 2¾ ins.
Plate Diam. 10⅜ ins.
MARKS 'Opaque China' over 'B. B. & I.' in a scroll, printed in blue.
National Museum of Wales, Cardiff.

PLATE 107 Square Vegetable dish, printed in blue with Willow pattern.
SIZE 9½ ins square. Ht. 5 ins.
MARK Impressed Baker, Bevans and Irwin, enclosing 4.
Private collection.

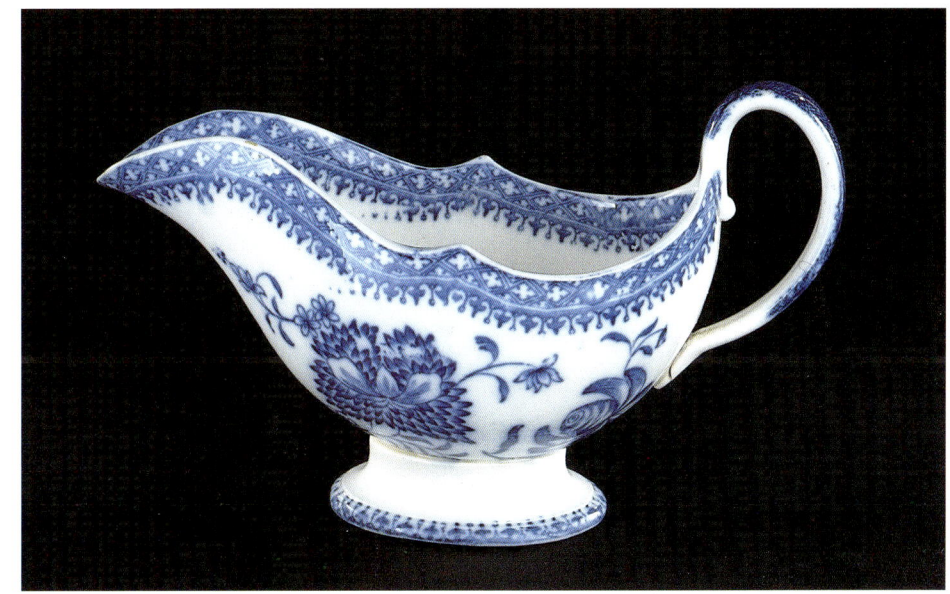

PLATE 108 Rare Sauce boat, printed in blue with stylised floral pattern. Unrecorded shape.
SIZE L. 7¾ ins. Ht. 4½ ins.
MARK None.   Private collection.

PLATE 109 Strainer, printed in blue with stylised floral pattern.
SIZE L. 10¾ ins.
MARK Impressed triangle △ and number 12.
Private collection.

PLATE 110 Miniature plate, with gadrooned edge, printed in sepia with shells and flowers pattern.
SIZES Diam. 4½ ins.
MARKS No mark.
Private collection.

PLATE 111 Arcaded or pierced Dessert plate printed in blue with Floral pattern. (It is most unusual to find these plates transfer printed).
SIZE Diam. 7½ ins.
MARK 'Opaque China' over 'B. B. & I.' in a scroll, printed in blue.
Private collection.

PLATE 112 Rare Mustard Pot and Cover, with gadrooned edge, printed in blue with Shells and Flowers pattern.
SIZE Ht. 3⅞ ins. Diam. 3½ ins.
MARK No mark.
National Museum of Wales, Cardiff.

PLATE 113 Oval Dessert Dish, printed in blue with Castle Gatehouse pattern.
SIZE L. 12½ ins. W. 9 ins.
MARK 'Opaque China' printed over 'B. B. & I.' in a scroll. Impressed 5.
Swansea Museum, Swansea City Council.

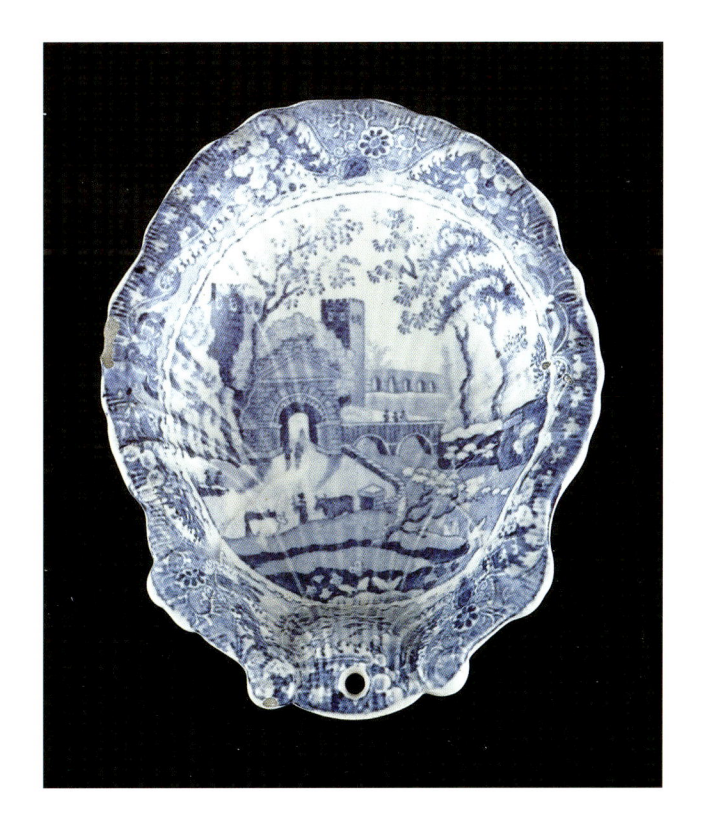

PLATE 114 Rare Pickle Dish, shell shaped, printed in blue with Castle Gatehouse pattern.
SIZE L. 5¾ ins W. 4¾ ins.
MARK 'Opaque China' over 'B. B. & I.' in a scroll, printed in blue.
Glynn Vivian Art Gallery, Swansea City Council.

115

PLATE 115/116 Rare Pierced basket with stand, printed in blue with The Ladies of Llangollen pattern. Unrecorded shape.
SIZE L. 10 ins. W. 6½ ins. Ht. 3¾ ins. Stand, L. 10½ ins.
MARK No Mark.
Private collection.

This mould seems to have been later used at The Llanelly Pottery, with different applied handles. For similar shape, see marked stand, Plate 95.

116

JUGS

Moulded Jugs

The 'Glamorgan' shape jug which occurs in many sizes, has the following characteristics: scalloped rim with ornate scroll moulding beneath the spout and handle, gadrooned decoration around the rim and shoulders, with a scroll handle and thumb rests. (The handle shape does vary).

PLATE 118 Moulded jug printed with Floral pattern, in black. The handle differs in having a 'strap' in the middle, with a pronounced 'spur' at the point of attachment at the top.
SIZE Ht. 6 ins.
MARK 'Opaque China' over 'B. B. & I.', printed in black.
Private collection.

PLATE 117 Moulded jug, printed in black with scenes from Rural Series. Mother and child with dog; Child feeding lamb.
SIZE Ht. 6¼ ins.
MARK 'Opaque China' over 'B. B. & I.', printed in black.
Swansea Museum, Swansea City Council.

PLATE 119 Moulded jug with unusual scale and floral relief mouldings under spout and handle, printed in black with Floral pattern.
SIZE Ht. 5½ ins.
MARK 'Opaque China' over 'B. B. & I.', printed in black.
Swansea Museum, Swansea City Council.

53

PLATE 120 Water Ewer with gadrooned decoration, printed in blue with the Tower pattern.
SIZE Ht. 11 ins.
MARK 'Opaque China' over 'B. B. & I.' in a scroll, printed in blue. Private collection.

Thrown Jugs
These also occur in a variety of sizes, usually transfer printed.

PLATE 121 Round jug, square shouldered handle, printed in blue with Pulteney Bridge, Bath pattern.
SIZE Ht. 5 ins.
MARK Transferers 2 in blue.
Private collection.

PLATE 122 Round jug and loop handle, printed in blue with vase of flowers, and overpainted in enamel colours.
SIZE Ht. 4¼ ins.
MARK No mark.
Private collection.

BREAKFAST and TEA WARES

The survival rate of pieces in every day use was obviously low, particularly with vulnerable shapes such as Cups, Tea and Coffee Pots and Cream Jugs. Hence, they are all extremely rare. Coffee pots appear in 3 distinct shapes, and although coffee cups were made (listed in Bryant's work book) none have been found. Their shape remains a mystery.

COFFEE POTS

PLATE 123 Coffee Pot of traditional shape, doomed lid, plain loop handle, printed in blue with Stylised Floral pattern. An early design. Unrecorded shape.
SIZE Ht. 9¾ ins.
MARK No mark.
Private collection.

PLATE 124 Globular coffee pot with moulded spout, doomed lid, loop handle with thumb rest, printed in blue, with Mandarin with Pipe pattern.
SIZE Ht. 8¾ ins.
MARK 'Opaque China' printed over 'B. B. & I.' in leafy scroll.
Glynn Vivian Art Gallery, Swansea.
This shape has also been found printed with the 'Vine' pattern.

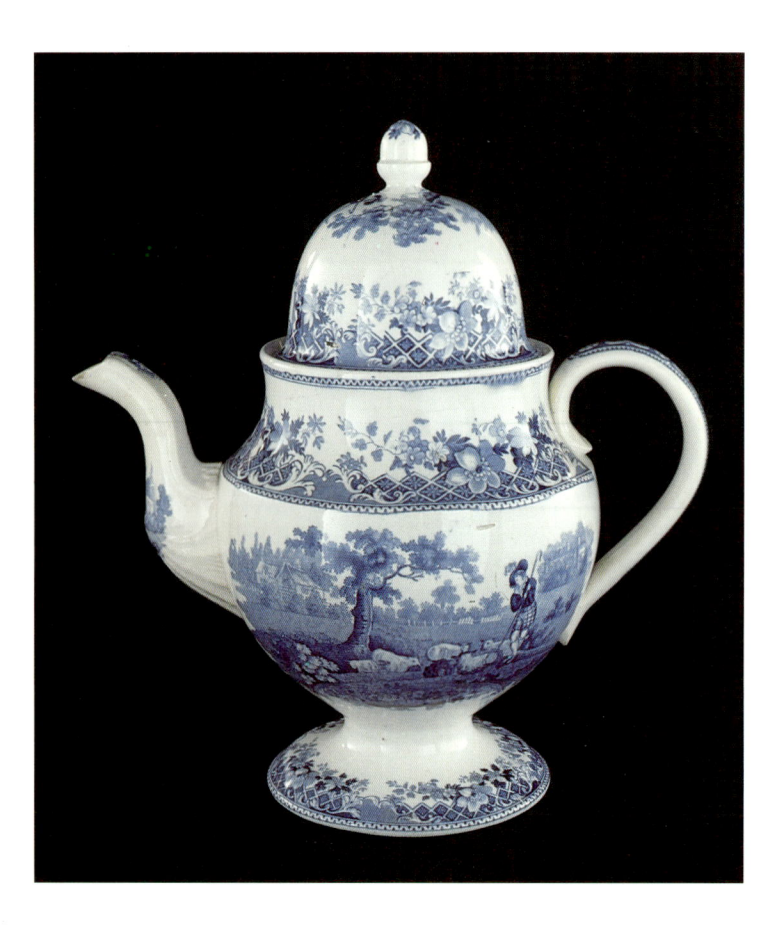

PLATE 125 Coffee pot, globular shape, with doomed lid, moulded spout, plain loop handle, printed in blue with Shepherd pattern.
SIZE Ht. 10 ins.
MARK 'Opaque China' over
'B. B. & I.' in a scroll. Private collection.

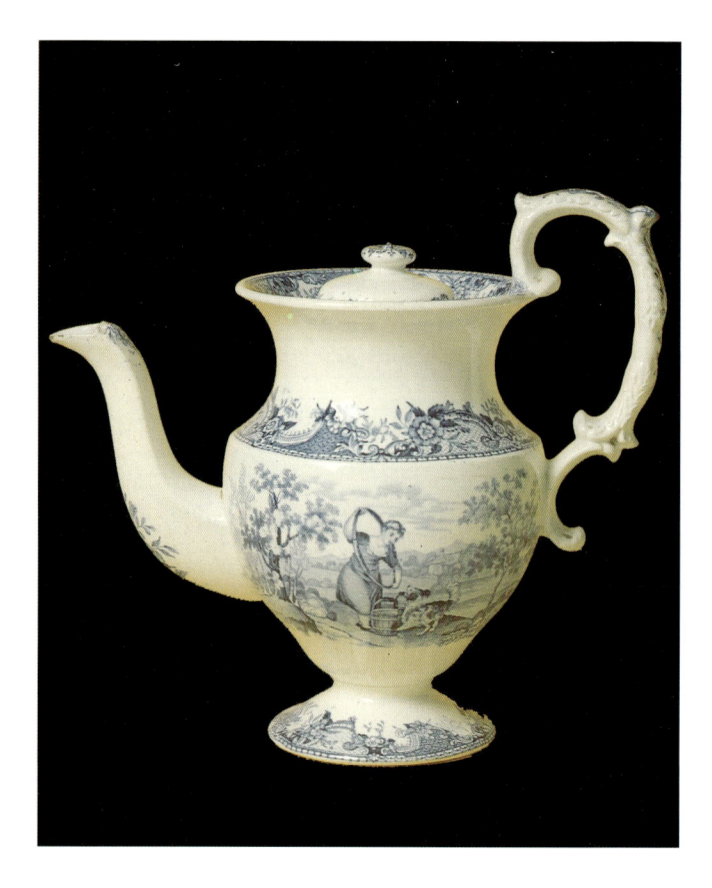

PLATE 126 Vase shaped coffee pot, with recessed lid and elaborate double scroll handle printed in blue with 'Cottage Girl' pattern. Unrecorded shape.
SIZE Ht. 8 ins to rim, 9½ ins to top of handle.
MARK No mark. Private collection.

TEAPOTS

PLATE 127 Globular teapot of early design, with high collar, plain loop handle and recessed lid. No mouldings. Printed in bue with 'Harper' pattern. Unrecorded shape.
SIZE Ht. 5 ins. L. 9¾ ins.
MARK Transferers 3 in blue. Private collection.

PLATE 128 Rectangular teapot, with castellated rim, ornate scroll handle, printed in blue with vase of flowers, overpainted in enamel colours. Unrecorded shape.
SIZE L. 10 ins. Ht. 5¾ ins.
MARK Impressed O.
Private collection.

PLATE 129 Large, rectangular Teapot, with high collar extending upwards to the front of the pot, strap handle, printed in blue with 'Cottage Girl' pattern. Unrecorded shape.
SIZE Ht. 7¾ins. L. 11¼ ins.
MARK No mark.
Private collection.

PLATE 130 Rounded teapot with collar extending upwards to front of pot, strap handle, printed in blue with Cowherd pattern. Unrecorded shape.
SIZE Ht. 6¼ ins. L. 10 ins.
MARK Impressed 15.
Private collection.

PLATE 131 Large rounded teapot with floral mouldings around rim. Small doomed lid, loop handle with thumb-rest. Printed in blue with 'Haymaker' pattern.
SIZE Ht. 7½ ins. L. 11 ins.
MARK Transferers 2 in blue.
Private collection.

PLATE 132 Teapot with indented sides, strap handle, and small doomed lid, printed in blue with Mandarin and Chinese Lantern pattern. The main body of the pot is transferred with the wide floral border of this pattern.
SIZE Ht. 7 ins. L. 11½ ins.
MARK 'Opaque China' over 'B. B. & I.', printed in a leafy scroll.
Private collection.

PLATE 134 Plain teapot, no mouldings, the handle distinctive in having a tightly curled scroll moulded termination. Printed in black with Fishing scenes from Rural Series.
SIZE Ht. 7 ins. L. 10½ ins.
Unrecorded shape.
MARK 'Opaque China' over 'B. B. & I.' in a scroll, printed in black.
Private collection. The cream jug, Plate 144 matches this teapot.

PLATE 133 Teapot with indented sides, strap handle and small doomed lid, but no collar, printed in blue with Shells and Flowers pattern. Unrecorded shape.
SIZE Diam. 6¾ ins. Ht. 5¾ ins.
MARK 'Opaque China' over 'B. B. & I.', printed in a scroll.
Private collection.

PLATE 135 Rounded teapot with floral mouldings applied around the scalloped high collar which extends up in front of the teapot. Scroll handle. Printed in black with Fishing scenes from Rural Series. Handle, spout and finial painted in black.
SIZE Ht. 6½ ins. L. 10 ins.
MARK 'Opaque China' over 'B. B. & I.' in a scroll, printed in black.
Swansea Museum, Swansea City Council.

SUGAR and SLOP BOWLS

PLATE 136 Sugar bowl with scalloped rim, printed in purple with 'Campania' pattern. Unrecorded shape.
SIZE Ht. 2¾ ins.
Diam. 5 ins.
MARK Transferer's 8 in purple.
Private collection.

PLATE 137 Sugar bowl and cover with moulded ring handles, printed in black with Fishing scenes from the Rural series. Unrecorded shape.
SIZE Ht. 4½ ins. Diam. 4¾ ins.
MARK 'Opaque China' over 'B. B. & I.', printed in a scroll.
Private collection.

PLATE 138 Slop bowl, printed in blue and overpainted in enamel colours. (Common shape).
SIZE Ht. 4¾ ins.
MARK Painter's squiggle in blue.
Private collection.

60

CREAM JUGS

PLATE 139 Small round cream jug printed in blue with stylised floral pattern.
Unrecorded shape.
SIZE Ht. 3¾ ins.
MARK No mark.   Private collection.

PLATE 140 Cream jug with indented sides on 4 paw feet, printed in pink with 'Vine' pattern.
SIZE Ht. 5¼ ins.
MARK 'Vine' over 'B. B. & I.' in a lattice and vine scroll.
Glynn Vivian Art Gallery, Swansea City Council.

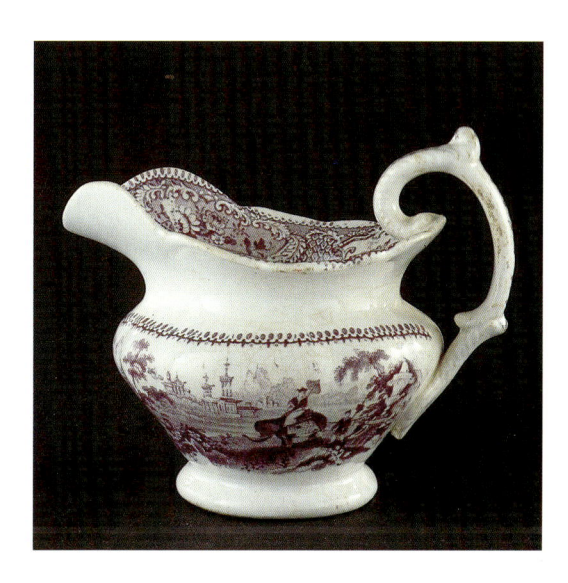

PLATE 141 Round cream jug with scalloped rim, printed in purple with 'Campania' pattern. The shape matches the marked Teapot illustrated in Nance Pl. XC (C), also the sugar bowl. Both unrecorded shapes.
SIZE Ht. 4 ins.
MARK Transferer's 8 in purple.
Private collection.

PLATE 142 Small round cream jug with wide elongated spout, printed in blue, overpainted in enamel colours.
Unrecorded shape.
SIZE Ht. 3¾ ins.
MARK Painter's dots in green.   Private collection.

61

PLATE 143 Cream jug with floral mounding around rim, printed in black with Rural series transfers.
SIZE Ht. 4½ ins. L. 6 ins.
MARK 'Opaque China' over 'B. B. & I.' in a scroll, printed in black. Private collection.

PLATE 143 Rectangular cream jug, French shape, printed in black with Fishing scenes from Rural series.
SIZE Ht. 4¼ ins. L. 5¼ ins.
MARK 'Opaque China' over 'B. B. & I.', printed in black. Impressed O. Private collection.
For reverse print, see Rural Series Plate 68.

PLATE 144 Cream jug with wide mouthed spout, floral termination at bottom of handle, printed in black with Rural Series transfers. Unrecorded shape.
SIZE Ht. 4¾ ins. L. 5¾ ins.
MARK 'Opaque China' over 'B. B. & I.', printed in black, impressed O.
Swansea Museum, Swansea City Council.
This shape matches teapot, Plate 134.

CUPS and SAUCERS

PLATE 145 Cup of French shape, printed in black with Fishing scenes from Rural series. Saucer printed with garden scene, figures sitting under a pergola beside steps.
SIZE Cup, Ht. 2½ ins.
Diam. (Top) 4 ins.
Saucer, Diam. 5¾ ins.
MARK 'Opaque China' over 'B. B. & I,' in a scroll, printed black.
Private collection.

PLATE 146 Cup and saucer, of French shape, printed in pale blue with Mandarin with pipe pattern.
SIZE Cup, Ht. 2¾ ins. Diam (Top) 3¾ ins. Saucer, Diam. 5¾ ins.
MARK 'Opaque China' over 'B. B. & I.' in a leafy scroll. Impressed crown.
Private collection.

PLATE 147 Cup with gadrooned rim, Etruscan shaped handle, printed in pale blue with Shells and Flowers pattern. Unrecorded shape.
SIZE Cup, Ht. 2¼ ins. Diam, 4 ins; Saucer, Diam. 5¾ ins.
MARK 'Opaque China' over 'B. B. & I.' in a scroll, printed in blue.
Private collection.

PUBLISHER'S ERRATUM
Plate 148 (p.64) and Plate 154 (p.66)
should be transposed

PLATE 148 Cup and saucer with scalloped rim. Cup has shallow bowl, and scroll ring handle. Printed in green with 'Campania' pattern. Unrecorded shape.
SIZE Cup, Ht. 2¾ ins. Diam. (Top) 4 ins. Saucer, Diam. 6 ins.
MARK 'Campania' over 'B. B. & Co.' in a leafy scroll.
Private collection.

PLATE 149 Cup of low form, with scroll handle, printed in pink with 'Vine' pattern. Unrecorded shape.
SIZE Cup, Ht. 2 ins. Diam. (Top) 3⅝ ins; Saucer, Diam. 5¾ ins.
MARK 'Vine' over 'B. B. & I.' in a lattice and leaf scroll, printed in pink.
Glynn Vivian Art Gallery,
Swansea City Council.

MUGS

PLATE 150 Mug with indented sides and gadrooned rim and base, printed in blue with Bridge and Tower pattern.
SIZE Ht. 3 ins. Diam. (Top) 3¼ ins.
MARK 'Opaque China' over 'B. B. & I.' in a scroll, printed in blue. Private collection.

PLATE 151 Plain mug with double rim base, printed in blue with 'Broseley' pattern.
SIZE Ht. 3 ins. Diam. 3⅛ ins.
MARK 'Opaque China' over 'B. B. & I.' in a scroll, printed in blue.
Swansea Museum, Swansea City Council.

PLATE 152 Rare, circular, Egg-Cup Stand, printed in blue with Broseley pattern.
SIZE Diam. 6½ ins.
MARK Baker, Bevans and Irwin, impressed in horseshoe encircling 5. Transferer's 2 in blue.
National Museum of Wales, Cardiff.

TOILET WARES

Wash hand Water Jug and Bowl sets were commonplace in the Victorian household and these seem to have survived well, although often separated from their partners. Toothbrush boxes and soap boxes are however much rarer, while 'chamber pots' and 'spitting pots', (listed in Bryant's workbook) remain unrecorded.

PLATE 153 A selection of toilet wares, printed in blue and black with the Tower pattern. These all have gadrooned edges and mouldings, common features in Glamorgan wares.
SIZES Jug, Ht. 10 ins. Bowl, Diam. 13½ ins. Soap box, 5 ins by 4 ins. Toothbrush holder, 8 ins by 3⅜ ins.
MARK All pieces marked with the usual transferred 'Opaque China' over 'B. B. & I.'
National Museum of Wales, Cardiff.

PLATE 154 Water Jug and matching Bowl, no mouldings. Jug with wide mouth and squat shape. Printed in blue with the Pulteney Bridge, Bath pattern.
SIZE Jug, Ht. 9 ins; Bowl, Diam. 12½ ins.
MARK Impressed Baker, Bevans and Irwin, in a horseshoe.
Swansea Museum, Swansea City Council.

PLATES 155 & 156 A rare
FOOTBATH, transfer printed
in green with Castle
Gatehouse pattern on the
inside and Tower pattern on
the outside. (It is unusual to
have two patterns on one
piece).
SIZE Depth 9 ins,
Width 14 ins, Length 22 ins.
MARK 'Opaque China' over
'B. B. & I.' printed in green.
Private collection.

67

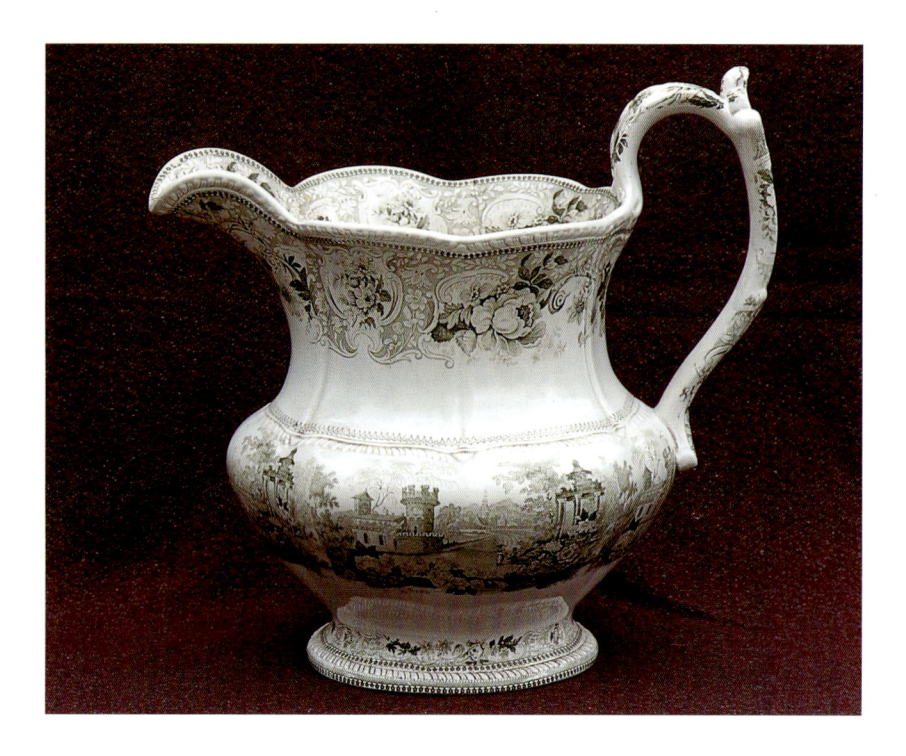

PLATE 157 A matching Water Jug of large proportions, printed in green.
SIZE Height 14½ ins.
MARK 'Opaque China' over 'B. B. & I.' printed in green.
Private collection.

PLATE 158 Water Jug of large proportions, with extra handle in the front for lifting and supporting, printed in black with the Tower pattern.
SIZE Ht. 14½ ins.
MARK 'Opaque China' over 'B. B. & I.', printed in black.
Private collection.

PLATE 159 Rectangular Toothbrush box, with canted corners, printed in blue with Broseley pattern.
Unrecorded shape.
SIZE L. 6¾ ins. W. 3 ins.
MARK Impressed Baker, Bevans and Irwin, in horseshoe, enclosing 1.
Private collection.

DECORATIVE OR ORNAMENTAL WARES

COW CREAMERS

Silver cow creamers were first imported from Holland in the early 18th century. The Staffordshire potteries copied the idea of using a cow as a container for cream around 1750, when the first saltglazed examples appeared. At Swansea, cow creamers were made both at the Cambrian and the Glamorgan potteries.

The bases measure about 4 ins to 5 ins in length by 3 ins in width and 4 ins in height. Each has a small lid on the back through which the jug was filled, the mouth acting as a spout, the tail a handle. The main difference in the moulds of the factories seems to lie not so much in the thickness of the base, which varies in both the Cambrian and Glamorgan examples, but in the shape of the breastbone (Brisket) between the front legs of the mould. In the Cambrian models, this is very pronounced, and protrudes downwards to a greater extent than in the Glamorgan cows, where it appears flatter, (See Pl. 162). Generally, the Glamorgan cows tend to have a more slender appearance with a squarer head. The commonest examples are those transfer-printed in black with rural fishing scenes depicted. They are invariably marked with the printed 'Opaque China' over 'B. B. & I.' in a scroll.

After examining numerous Swansea cows there seems to be only one other type of decoration which can be ascribed to the Glamorgan Pottery. These are plain, reddish brown glazed examples where the glaze lies thinly in parts to expose the finely modelled base. These floral bases can clearly be seen as an exact match to the marked examples. These seem to have been produced in fewer numbers. Interestingly, the 'Glamorgan Cow' was an old dairy breed of Welsh cattle, dark brown or mahogany in colour, now a rare breed. All the cows decorated in pink luster appear to be of Cambrian origin.

PLATE 160 Cow creamer printed in black with Fishing scenes from Rural series.
SIZE Length 6¾ ins. Base 4½ ins by 3⅛ ins.
MARK 'Opaque China' over 'B. B. & I.' in a scroll, printed in black.

PLATE 161 Cow creamer painted in brown.
SIZE Length 6¾ ins.
Base 4½ ins by 3⅛ ins.
MARK No mark.

PLATE 162
Cambrian cow in the centre flanked by Glamorgan cows, to show difference in the mould.

Plates 160 to 162
Glynn Vivian Art Gallery, Swansea City Council.

70

PUZZLE JUGS

Puzzle jugs were decorative items used on convivial occasions. The neck is ornamental with openwork piercing, thus making the jug unsuitable for normal use. Around the rim are 3 nozzles, all entering a tube which encircles the rim and leads into the hollow handle which extends to the base and opens into the interior of the jug. By covering all but one of the nozzles, it is possible to drink from the uncovered nozzle by suction. The 'puzzle' is that a small inconspicuous hole concealed in the handle also has to be covered in order to secure a drink!

The holes and patterns were punched out by hand with a sharp knife or a variety of different shaped punches. This type of work can also be clearly seen on pierced edge plates and the oval chestnut basket dish (Pl. 115/116). The laborious nature of the work often led to slips but the irregularity of some of the designs lends a certain charm to the pieces.

The shape and punched pattern of the Glamorgan puzzle jug, differs clearly from those of the Cambrian. The design is made up of a repeated pattern of 4 'heart' shapes separated by small, circular cut-out shapes.

PLATES 163/164 Rare Puzzle jug, printed in blue with Pulteney Bridge, Bath pattern.
SIZE Ht. 7½ ins. Diam across rim 4½ ins. Diam of base 4¾ins..
MARK No mark.
Glynn Vivian Art Gallery, Swansea City Council.

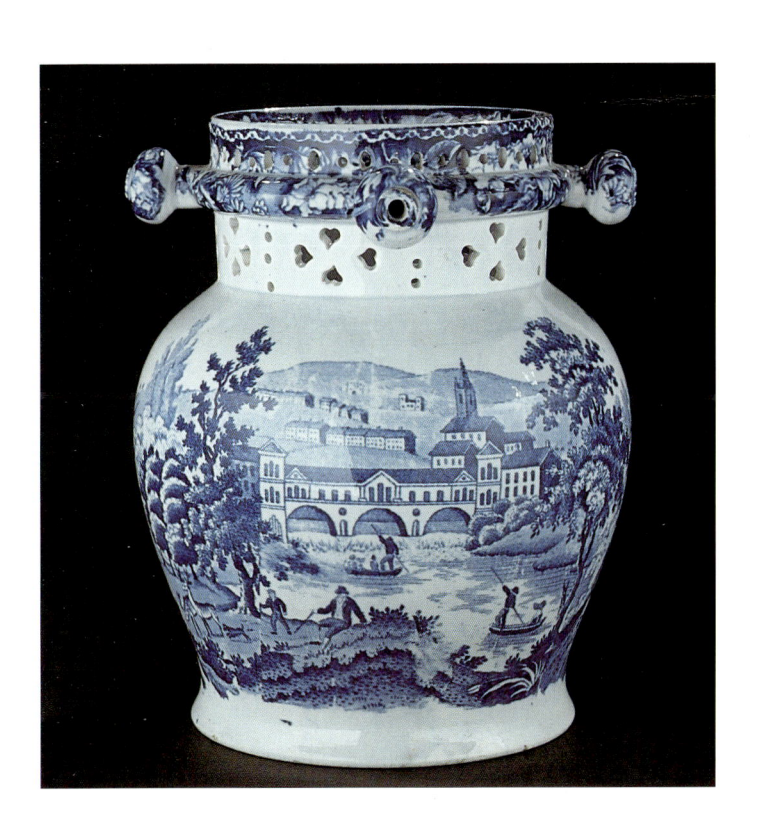

71

VASE

PLATE 165 Rare thistle shaped Vase printed in green with the Shells and Flowers pattern. (Similar vases were made at the Cambrian).
SIZE HT. 7 ins.
MARK 'Opaque China' over 'B. B. & I.' in a scroll, printed in green.
Swansea Museum, Swansea City Council.

MINIATURE PLATES

Miniature plates with unusual floral and scale moulding around the border are usually found with transfers from the Rural series.

PLATE 166 Miniature plate printed in black with Fishing scene from Rural series.
SIZE Diam. 6 ins.

Pl. 167

Pl. 168

Pl. 169

Pl. 170

Pl. 171

Pl. 172

MARKS

Impressed Marks

1. The earliest factory mark is the impressed BAKER, BEVANS & IRWIN in a horseshoe over the word SWANSEA in a straight line enclosing the Prince of Wales Feathers. See Pl. 167.

2. An impressed capital 'H' is also found on pottery of the pre-1820s period, obviously the mark of Haynes. The blue transferred stylised floral pattern which is always exceptionally well potted, usually bears this mark. See Pl. 167.

3. Impressed BAKER, BEVANS & IRWIN in a horseshoe often enclosing a number. See Pl. 168.

4. The impressed Prince of Wales Feathers mark may be found alone.

Transferred Marks

5. 'Opaque China' over the initials 'B. B. & I.' in an elaborate scroll. This appears to be the commonest mark. See Pl. 169.

6. 'Opaque China' over the initials 'B. B. & I.' in a branching leafy scroll. This mark occurs only on 'Mandarin' patterns. See Pl. 170.

7. 'GOTHIC BORDER' printed over the initials 'B. B. & I.' in a scroll. See Pl. 171.

8. 'Harper' over the initials, 'B. B. & I.' in a scroll. See Pl. 172.

9. 'Haymaker' over the initials 'B. B. & I.' in a scroll. See Pl. 173.

10. 'Campania' over the initials 'B. B. & Co.' in a leafy scroll (B. B. & Co. was only used on this pattern). See Pl. 174.

11. 'Cottage Girl' in a festoon over the initials 'B. B. & I.' See Pl. 175.

12. 'Vine' over the initials 'B. B. & I.' in an elaborate lattice and vine leaf scroll. See Pl. 176.

13. A unique method of marking pottery on the front of plates was employed at the Glamorgan on their design of early blue transfer printed ship subjects. The factory mark of 'G P Co / S' representing Glamorgan Pottery Company, Swansea, is incorporated into the bale of goods and the head of a barrel in the foreground of the ship patterns, in small, usually blurred letters. Similarly, the letter S for Swansea appears on Willow plates. See Pl. 93/94.

Transferers' numbers also occur in small numerals, usually printed in the same colour as the transfer.

Pressed Marks
14. An impressed 8 petalled daisy. See Pl. 177.
15. An impressed 6 pointed star.
16. An impressed Crown. See Pl. 178.
17. An impressed triangle.
18. An impressed Cross. See Pl. 179.
19. An impressed playing card 'Club' mark. ♣
20. An impressed Diamond. ◇
21. Impressed. ⬜

Painters' dashes and squiggles also occur on hand painted wares in any colour.

 The term 'Opaque China' had first been adopted or invented by Haynes in about 1790 at the Cambrian, before his partnership with Dillwyn, but there it was rarely used. Its subsequent usage at the Glamorgan was more than probably the suggestion of Haynes. The term was initially employed on fine white earthenware to suggest that it compared favourably with porcelain. While not absolutely unknown outside Swansea, the term has generally become accepted as a Glamorgan Pottery mark, but it must be emphasised that this is true only when accompanied by the transferred initials B. B. I. in a scroll, the commonest and most prevalent factory mark.

Pl. 173

Pl. 174

Pl. 175

Pl. 176

Pl. 177

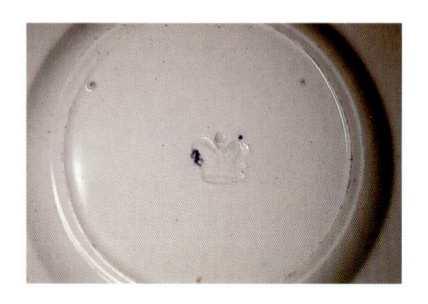

Pl. 178

Pl. 179

PRICES AND MEASURES

Many potteries, including the Glamorgan, united in the year 1813, under the name of a 'Chamber of Commerce', in order to prevent destructive price cutting. They set up a standard price fixing list by which all the ordinary ware was to be regulated—the scheme to commence on January 1st, 1814. This list of established prices standardised the typology, sizes and prices of pottery, and represented the potters' top wholesale prices. In 1814 the list was organised according to decoration rather than type of ware, thus prices per dozen for a 10in. plate varied from 'cream coloured ware', 1/6d; 'Willow ware', 4/-, to 'Transfer printed ware' being the most expensive at 5/- per dozen. These low charges reflect a correspondingly low rate of wage.

'Potter's Dozen'.
The curious 'dozens' of 12, 18, 24, etc. are explained in a pamphlet of 1840 called 'The ruin of potters and the way to avoid it—addressed to the consideration of all in the trade by a manufacturer', (that manufacturer being Wedgwood).

The rule was determined by the size of a pint mug, by all articles which were deemed 'hollow ware' of whatever shape. Those containing 1 pint were counted as twelve to the dozen. If they contained less, the quantity was increased; if more, the quantity diminished. Thus 'covered bowls' listed on the schedule form of Job Bentley (Appendix I), would vary from 18, 24, 30 and 36 to 'count 12' depending on the volume of liquid they contained.

Dishes, plates etc., generally denominated 'flatware' had their value estimated according to the number of inches they measured—most kinds of table and dessert ware had their value fixed in this way.

In order to compete with prices, however, the potters could give extra measure, while apparently abiding by the rules generally agreed on by the Chamber of Commerce. It was widely known that 'Spode's "pint" jugs held 3 half pints and that J. Ridgeway made larger wares than anyone.' Nothing could prevent one potter from making his size larger than another's.

Chapter 7

THE HAYNES FAMILY

The first child born to George and Catherine Haynes was Hannah, in 1781, and their second, Felicia, in 1787. A year after their arrival at Swansea, George's wife Catherine gave birth to their first son, George (1790). In 1793 a second son, William Woodward, was born. The family was now complete with two daughters and two sons.

HANNAH HAYNES 1781-1835
George and Catherine's first daughter Hannah moved with her parents to Swansea from Warwickshire aged eight years. On the second of May 1809 she married William Baker, son of Mary and James Baker, at St Mary's parish church, Swansea. The Baker family (relatives by marriage to the Haynes) were also from Henley-in-Arden and had moved to Swansea at about the same time as the Haynes. William Baker had gained much experience in the business of potting at the Cambrian pottery where he was employed as his father-in-law's assistant. By 1814 the new Glamorgan pottery was in operation with William Baker as its principal proprietor and manager, an appointment most certainly made under the auspices of Haynes. Sadly, after only ten years of marriage, William died (aged forty eight); he was described as a 'man of versatile gifts, whose character was widely esteemed'. Hannah was now forced into the position of taking control of her husband's business interests and acted out her husband's role as chief partner. This position she held until her death in 1835. Her address at this time is recorded as Nelson Place, Swansea, a row of houses which ran alongside the Western end of St. Mary's Church—recently demolished for the builidng of the new Quadrant Shopping Centre. There are no records of any children.

FELICIA HAYNES b.1787
George and Catherine's second daughter, Felicia, seems to have been the only one of the four children not to have shared in any of the family's business affairs. She

married Samuel-Fox Parsons of Cwmdwr, Clydach, at Llangyfelach church on May the 10th, 1819. The families at this time had neighbouring residencies (see map) and would probably have met due to the close proximity of the properties. Her husband soon entered into the Haynes family business, becoming a partner in the Glamorgan pottery. They had two children, Sarah and John, both baptised at Llangyfelach Parish Church. The family are recorded as residing at Picton Place, Swansea (now part of the lower Kingsway, Swansea), an area of large prestigious houses in the centre of the town.

GEORGE HAYNES JNR. 1790-1849

George Haynes junior had many business interests in Swansea. From the year 1816 he joined his father in his banking business at Wind Street, Swansea ('Haynes and son'). Later he became a junior partner in his father's banks at Neath and Llanelli. In 1810 George became secretary of the Public Rooms which their bank had financed and been instrumental in building. He was a senior partner in the Cambrian Porter brewery in the Strand, and, after 1817, became a shareholder in the Cambrian pottery, in partnership with Bevington and Co., doubtless at this time guided by his father's earlier experience at the Cambrian.

His home at this time was Burrows Lodge, Swansea, a house built originally in 1800 for George Jones Esq. By the year 1826, George was certainly living here as *The Swansea Guide* of that year notes, 'Burrows Lodge, the seat of G. Haynes Junior Esq.' The Leisure Centre now stands on the site of the house which was demolished in 1959.

In 1826 the Haynes and Co. banking firms were declared bankrupt (see Chapter 8) which must have left George Haynes junior financially embarrassed. During July and August of 1827 several sales were held at Burrows Lodge Swansea, of his furniture, china and books. The sales were attended by L. W. Dillwyn who in fact made several purchases, including pottery, which he records in his diary: 'bought a good deal of my own making'.

After the death of his wife Jane (nee Hopkinson) in 1829, George left Swansea with his three children, Emily, George and Jane. He seems to have travelled abroad, certainly living in Trieste, then part of Austria. Trieste, standing at the head of the Adriatic sea, was the trade outlet for all of central Europe in the nineteenth century, based chiefly on its port. This would have lent itself to many business opportunities for George. Here at Trieste a daughter, Francis, was born to George by his second marriage to Dorothea (of London).

The Bath chronicle of the twelfth of January 1849 records in the notices of deaths 'twenty first of January in Pulteney Street in this city, George Haynes Esq.: late a merchant of Trieste'. The household occupants in the census of 1851 showed that at his house at 14 Pulteney Street lived his widowed wife Dorothea and two daughters—Jane, twenty four, unmarried, born in Swansea, and Francis, thirteen, scholar, born in Austria. The family had the services of a parlour maid, cook and housemaid. Whatever business ventures George had entered into after leaving Swansea, they must have proved favourable.

(A birth out of wedlock was recorded at St Mary's Church, in Feb. 1812 to a Mary Lewis, of Swansea, naming George Haynes Jnr. as father)

WILLIAM WOODWARD HAYNES b. 1793

William, the youngest child, had with his parents enjoyed the company of the Collins family of Oxwich from a very early age. The Reverend John Collins, rector of Oxwich church, a graduate of Oxford, had married Ann (nee Wells), the daughter of a local wealthy family. He farmed his own land and was well supplied with produce from his tithe income. Collins kept a set of diaries between the years 1781-1811, where his daily expenses were recorded on one page and his family's social life on the other. These records show that not only was Collins a long standing customer of the Cambrian pottery, but also a close friend of George Haynes. The Haynes family visited the parsonage frequently and the two families were eventually united by the marriage of William Woodward to the rector's youngest daughter, Ann Collins (Nanny), in 1826. They had three children: Katherine, George Baker and John Wells. Their eldest son, George Baker Haynes, became Registrar of Births, Marriages and Deaths in Swansea for many years. In his possession was an oil painting, one of a pair commissioned possibly by the Reverend John Collins or by George Haynes and certainly the work of Thomas

THE HAYNES FAMILY

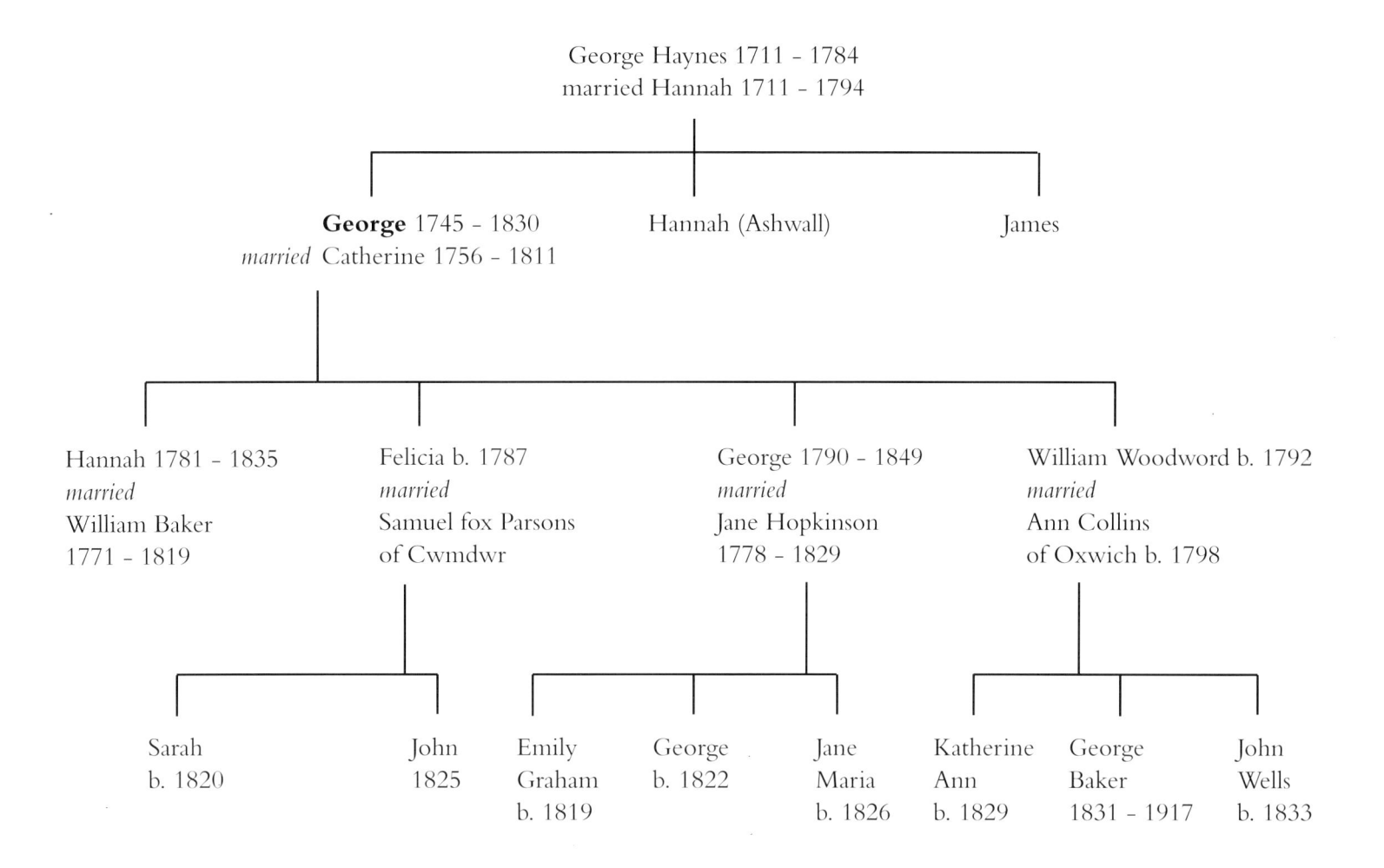

George Haynes 1711 – 1784
married Hannah 1711 – 1794

- **George** 1745 – 1830
  married Catherine 1756 – 1811
- Hannah (Ashwall)
- James

Children of George and Catherine:

- Hannah 1781 – 1835 *married* William Baker 1771 – 1819
  - Sarah b. 1820
  - John 1825
- Felicia b. 1787 *married* Samuel fox Parsons of Cwmdwr
  - Emily Graham b. 1819
- George 1790 – 1849 *married* Jane Hopkinson 1778 – 1829
  - George b. 1822
  - Jane Maria b. 1826
- William Woodword b. 1792 *married* Ann Collins of Oxwich b. 1798
  - Katherine Ann b. 1829
  - George Baker 1831 – 1917
  - John Wells b. 1833

Rothwell, the engraver and artist at the Cambrian pottery. The work is now housed at Swansea Museum. It is believed that both George Haynes and Collins appear in the open carriage. A figure in black with clerical wig has been identified as Collins, the other gentleman in red coat and wearing a black Tricorn hat is in all probability George Haynes (attribution by Mike Gibbs).

George Haynes was one of few gentlemen in Swansea who possessed a chaise. The carriage appears to be driven along the sand road which led from the dunes of Oxwich Bay up into Nicholaston village and then on to Swansea, this being the quickest route into the town.

William Woodward became a partner in the Glamorgan Pottery after 1819 and remained so until its closure in 1838. He was also a partner with his father and brother in the Neath branch of the bank 'Haynes and Co.' In 1825 he became a freeman by virtue of his father-in-law also having been a freeman, and in 1830, he was appointed collector and inspector of the new market in Swansea.

The Haynes family Tombstone in St Mary's Church, Swansea, reads:

> In memory of
> Hannah Haynes, widow,
> Relict of Geo. Haynes of
> Henley in Arden, Warwicks.
> Gentle. who Died 26 November,
> 1794 Aged 83 years.
> Also of Mrs. Mary Baker, Widow,
> Of the late Mr. James Baker of
> Henley in Arden, who died on
> 25 Octr. 1805, aged 64 years.
> Also of Catherine, wife of Mr.
> Geo. Haynes of this town who died
> 11th Octr. 1811 Aged 55 years
> Also of William Baker, born 27th July
> 1771, died 15th June 1819. Aged 47 years
> Also of Mrs. Mary Haynes, wife of
> George Haynes. Born 8 Sept 1779. Died
> 29th Mar. 1829. Aged 49 years
> Also of George Haynes, Born 9th Sept
> New Stile 1745 Died 2nd Janry. 1830 Aged 85 years.
> Also of Hannah Baker Baker, relict of the
> Above named William Baker. Died April 17th 1835
> Aged 64 years

Chapter 8

GEORGE HAYNES—HIS OTHER INTERESTS

Although Haynes's career prior to his arrival at Swansea remains a mystery, his business interests after his removal to South Wales were to become very diverse and well-known. He was clearly a man of ability in the most varied of forms, coupled with a strong devotion to public duty. Consequently his life was to leave a lasting impression on the town of Swansea. He and his family were loyal and steadfast churchgoers, his elder son, George Haynes Jnr, holding the post of church warden at St Mary's Parish Church between 1818 and 1819. The family's contribution of pews to the church was described in St Mary's Church Daybook as 'superior accomodation' and it was noted that they also made provision for 'substantial and appropriate repairs'. At the time of the founding of the Glamorgan Pottery (1814), George Haynes was one of the leading businessmen in the town and undoubtedly a prominent figure in all public matters, supporting many local charities and causes.

BANKING

From about 1800 Haynes had been associated with the Swansea banking firm of which Henry Pocklington was senior partner. After Pocklington's death in 1816, George Haynes junior joined his father and continued their banking partnership alone as 'Haynes and Son'. Their bank was situated in Wind Street and was one of three banks in the town. It was this bank which financed the establishment of the Glamorgan Pottery. George and his son also partly owned the Banking firm of 'Haynes, Day, Haynes and Lawrence' in Llanelli—this was certainly in existence by 1823. Two other branches were in operation in Llandeilo and Hay. In 1820, the Bank of 'Haynes and Co' opened in Neath, the partners being George Haynes senior, George Haynes junior and William Woodward Haynes, the youngest son.

On 18th July 1805 a meeting was held at The Bush Inn, High St, Swansea, of intending subscribers towards erecting Public rooms and a theatre, where it was resolved that the subscribers should form themselves into a body by the name of 'The Swansea Tontine Society'. Amongst the list of names of promoters were George Haynes and L. W. Dillwyn, who agreed on five shares each. The outcome of this meeting was the building of The Theatre Royal on the corner of Temple St. and Goat St. (demolished 1899) and the erection of the Assembly Rooms in Cambrian Place which still remain. By 1810, George Haynes was secretary of this society, with his Swansea branch of Haynes and Co. acting as treasurers. He became actively engaged in raising subscriptions 'by way of Tontine in the shares of five pounds each for erecting Public Rooms at the Burrows.' The Burrows was an area south of Wind Street, adjacent to the Bay and Harbour entrance and now known as Somerset Place and Gloucester Place. It was one of Swansea's prestigious areas in the early nineteenth century, and popular with visitors. The Public Rooms were to serve as a further attraction and advantage to the town.

Matthew's *Directory* of 1816 names Haynes also as treasurer of Swansea's Savings Bank and treasurer of 'the Royal Swansea Lancastrian Free School' in Goat Street - a grammar school for 300 boys. The school was founded on Lancastrian principles in which the 'reading of the Bible was introduced without notice or comment, thus excluding no sect or party'. The school was supported by voluntary donations and subscriptions, children being recommended by subscribers.

One pound banknote issued by the Swansea branch of George Haynes & George Haynes Jnr. 1822.
By permission of the National Museum of Wales, Welsh Folk Museum, St. Fagan's, Cardiff.

The Collapse of the Swansea Banks

The years 1825/6 brought a financial crisis which disrupted the banking business in Swansea as in many other places up and down the country. The Haynes banks, like so many others, were forced to close their doors—at Swansea, Llandeilo, Hay and Neath. Their banknotes became worthless and that is probably why several have survived.

Public meetings in Swansea, immediately after the failure, expressed confidence in the bank of Haynes and Co., and by 24th of December, 1825, 'a few gentlemen and the Trade of the Town of Swansea gave guarantees totalling £35,000 for it', although eventually the Bank could only pay seven shillings and two pence in the pound. The failure of the banks in Swansea 'threw the whole town and neighbourhood into a state of indescribable consternation and distress', the alarm being intensified by the crash of banks in London and throughout the country. By February 1826 Lewis Weston Dillwyn had been called on to settle about two hundred disputes arising from the failure of masters to pay their workmen. The difficulties continued until the April or later of the following year, and it was not until the May of 1826 that £3,000 was sent in silver by the 'Government' to the collector of Excise in Swansea to alleviate the situation.

Haynes's banks never re-opened their doors. George Haynes senior (now aged eighty one) would not have been actively engaged in the business of banking at this time, but the affairs were probably managed by his sons George and William Woodward. On 23rd October, 1826 the new Bank of England Branch Bank at Swansea opened for business following upon the petitions of influential businessmen in the locality.

HAYNES AND THE SWANSEA HARBOUR AND CANAL

In 1790 an Act of Parliament was passed by virtue of which the Swansea Harbour Trust was constituted. It was an Act 'for repairing, enlarging and preserving the Harbour of Swansea'. The trustees appointed were to be representative of all the various interests in the Port and comprised the following:—Duke of Beaufort and Son; the Lords Stewards; Recorder; Water bailiff; Coroner and Bailiff of the Seigniories; Marquis of Worcester;

Sir Herbert Mackworth; the Portreeve and Aldermen of the town of Swansea; and twelve of the Burgesses of the borough, which included 'George Haynes of the pottery'.

These persons formed the first trustees. Re-election of members took place annually and George Haynes's name continued to appear as a trustee at meetings held at the Guildhall for the next fourteen years, until 1804. His name also appears with regularity throughout these years on subcommittees of an investigative nature. The duties of the trustees were extensive, and the powers conferred upon them included those of construction of docks, piers, and the charging of tolls and dues. Improvements to the harbour proceeded immediately after the formation of the Trust. The river was cleaned, widened and deepened, a beacon or lighthouse was erected on the Mumbles Head for the guidance of vessels entering the port, and two stone piers were erected at the entrance to the harbour. As a result of these improvements, vessels of up to 300 tons were enabled to enter and leave the harbour on the lowest neap tides. The Duke of Beaufort and the Swansea Corporation duly received fees and tolls in respect of all shipping entering the port of Swansea.

By May of 1799 debts of the trustees were 'very pressing' and it was ordered that 'no new erection was to be proceeded until the debts were liquidated'. Several local benefactors came to the aid of the trust: George Haynes's contribution was a subscription for the sum of £25 'to be applied to the boundary of the back wall of the pier'. In 1804 he also bequeathed ten guineas towards defending the harbour against French attack.

A few years after the Harbour Trust came into operation, another Act of Parliament was passed on May 23rd, 1794—'for making and maintaining a navigable Canal from the Town of Swansea to the Parish of Ystradgynlais in the County of Brecon'. The proposals were for a narrow canal which would be best adapted to the narrow valley through which it would pass. Barges of up to seventy feet in length and seven to seven and a half feet in breadth would be able to carry loads of up to twenty tons. To accommodate these boats, the canal would be thirty feet wide and five feet deep.

The growing export of local coal and import of ores for the expanding copper industry at the end of the eighteenth century required both improved port facilities and the development of communication from inland to the port, if Swansea was to become an industrial town. The canal did much to meet these needs, bringing many of the upland districts of the valleys into touch with the port. The canal was finally completed by 1798, sixteen miles in length with thirty six locks and rising nearly four hundred feet along its length. Trade within the port of Swansea thus quadrupled within ten years of the canal being built.

The Canal Navigation Assembly minute book of 1794 records that a meeting was held at the Mackworth Arms, High Street, Swansea to elect a committee. Messrs Coles and Haynes's names appear as two of the elected members, although Haynes's name appears solely at subsequent meetings throughout the period of 1794-1822 for John Coles lived at Gloucester and took no active part in local affairs.

George Haynes's interests in the canal were both as a private individual who used the services of the canal for the transport of goods to and from his home at Ynystanglwys House, Clydach (after 1811) and also as a commercial customer. Canal account ledgers record that there were two accounts payable by G Haynes, the private account for his home and a second account appearing under the heading 'Swansea' from the year 1813 (when the Glamorgan Pottery became operational). Rent was paid by him to the Swansea Canal Navigation in the form of tolls and wharf charges—the rate in 1817 being a half pence per ton per mile.

THE LIBRARY
The year 1804 saw the formation of the Glamorgan library in Wind Street, Swansea—the first public library in the town. It was established and administered out of funds from members by way of subscription and entrance fees. Such a library belonged to the entire membership and its affairs were managed by a committee. George Haynes was one of its founders. By 1808, the proprietors numbered thirty. Historical, classic and topographical subjects were predominant along with natural history, law, travel, drama, poetry and English literature. *The Cambrian* records in July 1805 'the recent establishment in this town of a public library must prove an invaluable acquisition, not only to the

inhabitants but to the numerous occasional residents of the town'. The rules required that 'novels shall be excluded' and that 'books on law, physic, or divinity should be subjected to a quarterly ballot of proprietors.' A librarian was appointed and given a salary on condition that 'he find a room for the books and provided a fire from Sept. 20th to March 20th!'

THE BREWERY

In September 1805 a Mr Henry Bonham signed his lease of the brewery and Wharf situated half way up the Strand to George Haynes. Here he continued the business of brewing along with his son, George, who was later to take over its management. The Cambrian Brewery was reportedly carried on by Messrs. Haynes and Co. and it was claimed by *The Swansea Guide* that they brewed 'excellent porter ale and beer for home consumption and exportation'.

THE SWANSEA VOLUNTEERS

During the year 1794, when Great Britain found itself at war with France, the government became very concerned about the extensive military preparations taking place on the French Channel coast—activities which were obviously directed towards an invasion of Britain. The problem of strengthening the land forces available to the government for home defence was remedied by authorising, in 1794, the raising of a Voluntary Corps to be used for defence of the kingdom. There followed a considerable response which led to the formation of Voluntary Corps, Infantry, Artillery and Light Horse or Yeomenry Cavalry.

One of the groups raised in Swansea was that of The Western Glamorgan Infantry Volunteers between 1803 and 1808. Here George Haynes held the senior rank of Captain, serving under the command of Lt. Colonel John Llewellyn of Penllergaer. The role of the Volunteer Corps in Swansea was primarily the defence of the town against the worst attentions of Napoleon. By the early 1800s, Swansea and the South Wales coastline was ready for instant action against the imminent invasion by the French.

A Cambrian pottery brown glazed jug inscribed 'Swansea Volunteers' in greenish black script is kept at the National Museum of Wales, Cardiff and was possibly commissioned by, or for, Haynes in his role as Captain at that time.

HAYNES AND *THE CAMBRIAN* NEWSPAPER

In 1804 a new chapter in the history of printing in Wales was commenced, for by Saturday, January 28th 1804, Thomas Jenkins of Wind Street, Swansea had printed and published the first edition of the first newspaper in Wales. Its name, heading its first page, was *The Cambrian and General Weekly Advertiser for the Principality of Wales*. The print, date and price, as found after the name were 'Printed and Published by T. Jenkins, Swansea, Glamorgan, January 28th 1804. (Price Sixpence).'

In the previous year of 1803, a proprietor had been sought and found for publishing the first English newspaper in the Principality. Mr George Haynes, who had just then returned from America, was the first to propose the formation of the company of shareholders for this purpose, the company to consist of one hundred £25 shares. The £2,500 was duly raised. After receiving various offers in answer to the advertisement published in the *Gloucester Journal* (this was the only paper in which county advertisements for South Wales were inserted), the company appointed Mr Thomas Jenkins of Swansea as editor and manager of *The Cambrian*.

The Cambrian was a great venture, beset from the outset with risks and difficulties, but Haynes duly overcame them. On the first page of the first issue George Haynes's address read thus,

> **To the public**, We deem it our duty to account for the non-publication of *The Cambrian* on the 7th instant, the period originally proposed and partially announced throughout the Principality - the delay arose from the circumstance of the chief part of our Printing Materials having been shipped at Bristol on board the PHOENIX SLOOP, Captain Diamond, bound for Swansea, which was in the first instance detained several days in the former port by contrary winds and when she had at length finally sailed, encountered a violent gale, which forced her into Milford, from whence she did not arrive until the 6th of this month, and we could not obtain our goods until the 12th...

A copy of the original prospectus is preserved at the Swansea museum. It advertises the paper as 'the first and only newspaper printed in Wales . . . which will be published on Sat. Jan 7th 1804 . . . and continued weekly, price Sixpence.' Thomas Jenkins partly owned, edited and printed the paper at his premises in Wind Street. In the 18th century the small, sparse population of Swansea had been supplied by London, Bristol, Hereford and Gloucester newspapers, though probably not adequately for the range of the town's interests even then. By the 19th century better roads, more frequent mail, denser settlements at the ports, market towns and summer resorts, called for a paper that would do more to reflect life in this busy part of Wales. Manufacturers, shippers, merchants, professional men and others, welcomed a local paper which would carry their advertisements, make known their case when parliamentary bills or petitions were in dispute, and generally foster the cause of 'improvement'. Others looked to a local paper to propagate their religious or political views. There were a number of incentives therefore to encourage the founding of a newspaper.

Initially the paper was fraught with difficulties such as heavy taxation, suspicion and hostility from the ruling class. News could be printed legally only on stamped sheets of prescribed size issued by the Stamp office. In 1797 the duty was three and a half pence for each copy. Paper itself was also taxed—each sheet costing nearly one penny. It was these regulations which determined the price of the paper. Additionally the cost of printing materials and labour costs had to be met, which rendered the final selling price of the newspaper relatively high. This in turn restricted sales so the paper could only pay its way if it attracted a sufficient number of advertisers. *The Cambrian* succeeded because it filled 35-40% of its column space with advertisements.

Great care had to be taken to avoid publishing anything offensive or to place an attack on local magistrates. *The Cambrian* proved to be a cautious, inoffensive publication which seldom warranted prosecution for libel. Its success lay in its impartiality. It espoused no cause except 'The spirit of Improvement' and commercial enterprise. It avoided taking sides in parliamentary contests and was able to do this since Swansea was one of the eight boroughs which joined to return a member of Parliament. However, it offered the use of its space and print to all sides, providing they paid for insertions at the full advertising rate.

The early papers were printed on single sheets folded to form four pages. The printing offices kept only a small stock of type, which was set by hand slowly. To get the paper ready in time (for Sat. publication) to catch the mail coach, the outer pages 1-4 containing standard adverts, articles and earlier news were printed on Wednesday and the type broken up and redistributed for use in preparing the later news and adverts on the inner pages.

For national news, editors relied on the London dailies and some border county prints, selecting interesting articles as they came on the mail coach and sending their selections to the composing room. During the winter months, when snow, floods and storms at the Severn Passage delayed the running of the mail coaches, the paper would have to be made up with general articles and paragraphs which were kept in hand, at the ready.

Payment of the stamp duty entitled papers to free carriage by the mail but only on the roads along which the mail ran. Distribution was therefore poor. Papers were often left at taverns, farms and sub-post offices for collection. Nevertheless, despite the inefficiency of distribution, in Wales then, as in the rest of Britain, the newspaper helped to develop among an increasingly literate working class population a new radical opinion on a nation-wide scale.

In South Wales in particular, where the impact of industrialisation became increasingly marked after 1800, the influence of newspapers was especially significant. Despite all legal impediments the newspaper eventually extended to a wider and wider reading audience.

In 1822 George Haynes and son George sold their interest in *The Cambrian* after the death of T. Jenkins when a Mr. John Williams, newspaper correspondent originating from Llanelli, purchased shares in *The Cambrian* and by 1830 had purchased all the shares and freehold premises in Wind Street.

Chapter 9

THE YNYSTANGLWYS ESTATE

YNYSTANGLWYS

Haynes's involvement in the Cambrian pottery works ceased in 1810. Having reached the age of sixty six, he and his family decided to move out of Swansea in order to detach themselves from the ever increasing demands of the town. Plans began for the building of a new residence some distance up the valley in the village of Clydach. The diaries of the Reverend John Collins of Oxwich record that the Haynes were certainly in residence at Clydach by the June of 1811. On August 6, a party was held at the new house, perhaps a celebration of their arrival or completion of the house and gardens.

The Swansea Guide of 1813 notes that the town was 'daily increasing in size and population and promising to prove a town of considerable commercial consequence'. It was quite natural at this time for Haynes to feel his place was better distanced from the town. It was customary for the wealthy to move out of towns to more congenial surroundings and Haynes was certainly a man of means. The guide continues,

> at about four miles from Swansea is CLYDACH, a sweet romantic spot, where is the tasty retirement of Mr Haynes who has built some cottages in a style that adds peculiar beauties to the spot. Here is a very large walled enclosure with hot and cold greenhouses. It was formerly a garden but has lately been converted into a nursery, much for the accommodation of the country at large.

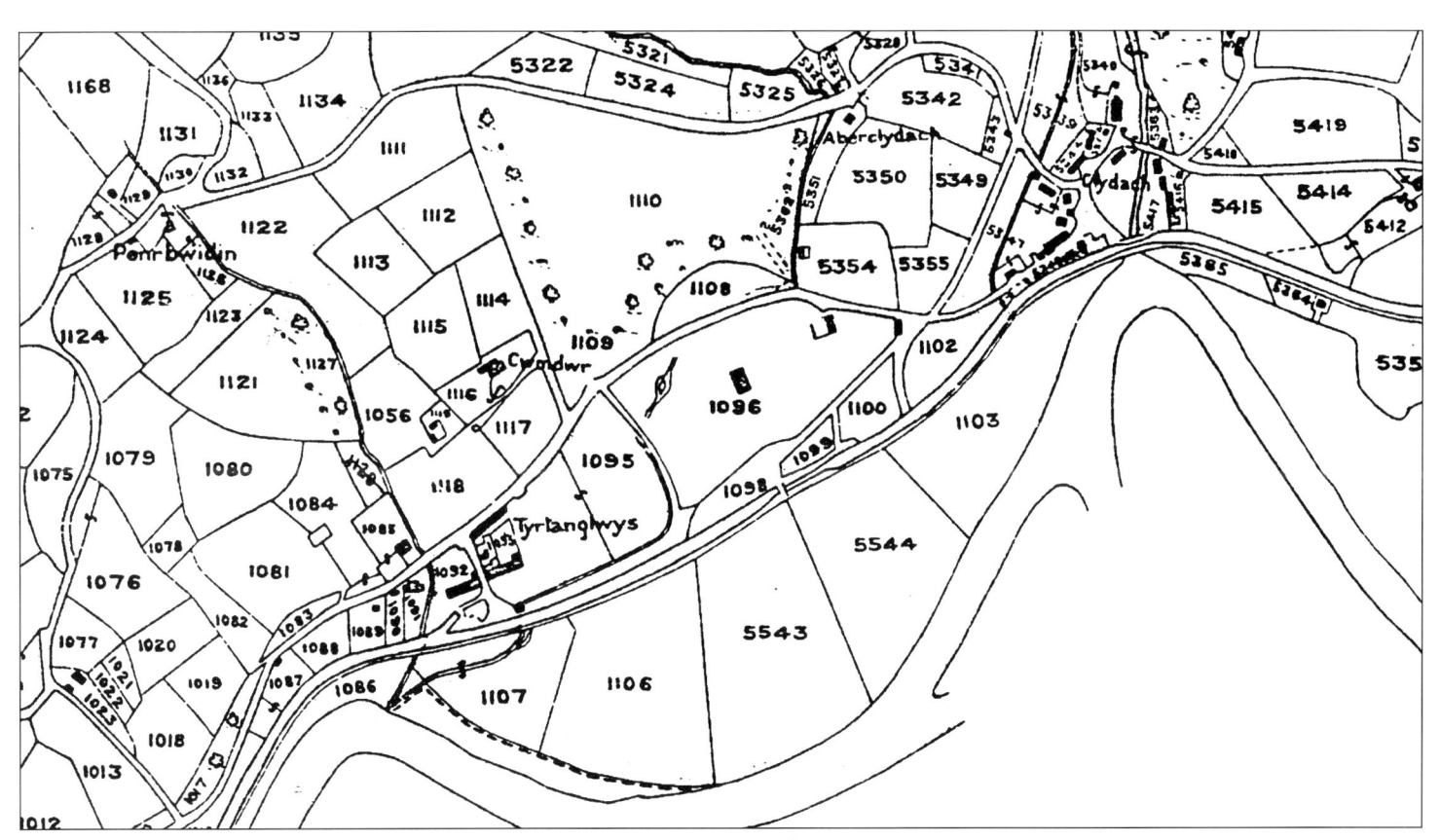

Tithe map of Llangyfelach parish, 1838, showing 'Tyrtanglwys' (Ynystanglwys) estate.
The estate was situated a mile or so south west of the village of Clydach and 6 miles or so north of Swansea. The Swansea valley canal ran through the property with wooded fields to the south, a walled garden and plantations to the north east. The turnpike road formed its boundary on the north, with further fields, underwood and plantations extending north of the road: in all 56 acres. 'Cwmdwr', the home of Samuel Fox Parsons, can be seen to the north, on the opposite side of the road.

Haynes, having apparently divorced himself from the business of the pottery and now 'out of sight' as it were in the small village of Clydach, set about creating for himself a pleasing environment as one of the landed élite. The simple lines of his Georgian house with gothic arched windows and long service wing behind, together with 6 new cottages, were built on the site of what must have been a farmhouse called Ynnistanglwys,[1] later spelled Ynystanglwys.

The estate was positioned between the main Swansea to Brecon turnpike road and the low lying land adjacent to the canal and river. *Ynys* is the Welsh word for 'an island or piece of land alongside a river,' or 'water meadow', 'Tanglwys' is a variant of the proper name Tangwystle—the name attested to a Saint, meaning Peace hostage.

The tithe map of 1837 which is here reproduced outlines the estate (then called 'Tyrtanglwys') which doubtless would have changed little in the few years after Haynes's death in 1830.

The house lay centrally in the estate, with a large plantation to the North of the Turnpike road, bordering on Cwmdwr property (home of the Fox Parsons) and several smaller plantations south of the canal. To the east of the house was a large parcel of land bordered by a high wall—a walled garden which must have been devoted to the production of vegetables and crops for use in the household and possibly of commercial benefit. Walled gardens were a common feature of the larger country home: they were built to offer protection from the wind and also to retain heat from the sun, they offered warm conditions where a large variety of crops

'Ynystanglwys', a watercolour painting of George Haynes's residence, near Clydach, Swansea, painted by J. Colguhoun 1914. The front of the house faces south, with workers' cottages to the south-east, bordering the canal.

Photograph by kind permission of Thomas Lloyd.

'Ynystanglwys' house, derelict in the 1940s. Although sad in appearance, it was clearly in need only of a superficial 'face-lift'.

could be grown. In a small field north of the house was an Ice-house. These were used widely in country houses in the late seventeenth and early eighteenth century; this was an early form of deep freeze, where perishable goods could be over-wintered. The site chosen was usually on a slope near a source of water, in this case the banks of the wooded area north of the Turnpike road where a natural stream drained water down from the hillside. Straw would have been used to insulate the walls and form layers between the ice which was packed around vegetables, fruit, meat and fish. The shade of the trees was cooling and therefore beneficial. Glasshouses and hot greenhouses also formed part of the estate.

Labourers' cottages were made a subordinate part of the scenery; there were six in all, adjacent to the main house and built to house the families who tended the estate, gardens and stables.

Tree planting was represented as a patriotic duty by many landowners. English hardwoods such as oak and elm together with Scots pine were particularly popular—evidence of this is seen in the water-colour painting of the house with a Scots pine in the foreground. Extensive plantations of rhododendron trees is still in evidence on the remains of the now deeply overgrown site. Transport improvements brought about by the Swansea valley canal which ran through the property and which had been actively supported by Haynes meant that goods were now readily transportable to and from his estate.

In total, the estate was estimated to contain fifty-six acres with gardens, stables, coach houses and outhouses, together with six cottages and gardens.

Sadly in October of 1811, George's wife, Catherine died, aged fifty five years. *The Cambrian* of October 12th, 1811 records, 'Early this morning, most seriously and deservedly regretted by her family and all who had the happiness of her society or acquaintance, Mrs Haynes, the much respected Lady of George Haynes Esquire of Swansea.'

The cottages and stables of Ynystanglwys estate. The view is from the canal path, the stables running parallel with the main turnpike Swansea to Brecon road.

On the twelfth of May 1814 George Haynes remarried—a Miss Mary Baker, at Llangyfelach parish church. George was to outlive his second wife also; she died in March 1829. A year later in the January of 1830, George Haynes died at his home, Ynystanglwys. He was buried at St Mary's Church, Swansea, where his tombstone still remains.

The estate at Ynystanglwys passed through several hands after Haynes's death, notably those of Illtyd Thomas of Glanmor, Swansea. In 1868, a portion of the estate was purchased by the Railway Company for the sum of £651. In 1925, John Player and sons purchased the remainder of the estate for £1,250. The cottages and houses were later split up and let for multiple occupation. The house was sadly demolished in 1946, the cottages later in the 1960s.

Epilogue

Several authors have attributed certain patterns, lustre pottery and other wares to the Glamorgan pottery, but where no evidence has been found to substantiate the information, I have not included them in this book.

It would be presumptuous to assume that every shape and pattern manufactured at the Glamorgan has been covered, but any new transfers or designs waiting to be discovered must be limited. The schedule of pottery shapes and sizes listed in Appendix II, indicates the extent of the wares produced, but many of these have unfortunately not yet been recorded. The author would welcome correspondence from fellow collectors, dealers or interested parties, on any new information which would help in the sharing of both knowledge and enjoyment.

Should this volume stimulate interest or further investigations, then its objective will have been achieved.

Note 1: 'An estate by the name of "Ynnistanglwys" in the parish of Llansamlet was in existence on this site in 1750. It was leased at that time to Evan Morgan of Cadaxton, Neath, at an annual rent of £40. In 1798 it was sold, purchasers unknown.' W. C. Rogers, *Swansea and Glamorgan Calendar*, Part 2, Vol. 3.

Selected Bibilography

BROOK, HENRY, *Monograph on the Tinplate Works in Britain*, 1932.

GRANT-DAVIDSON, D. J., 'Early Swansea Pottery 1764-1810', in *The Transactions of the English Ceramic circle, Vol. 7, Pt. 1* pp. 59-82, 1968.

DILLWYN, L. W., Diaries IX and X, also *Calendar of the Diary of L. W. Dillwyn, Vol. 11, Oct 1817-Nov. 1832* (Nat. Lib. of Wales).

DRAKARD and HOLDWAY, *Spode printed ware*, 1983.

EVANS, JOHN, *Letters written during a Tour through South Wales in 1803 and other times*, 1804.

FRANCIS, GRANT, *The Smelting of Copper in Swansea*, 1881.

GODDEN, G & GIBSON, M., *Collecting Lustre ware*, 1991.

GRIFFITHS, IVOR, 'A brief history of Ynyspenllwych', in *A History of Clydach*, 1901.

Guide to Swansea, 1813.

HAGGAR, MOUNTFORD and THOMAS, *The Staffordshire Pottery Industry*, 1967.

JENKINS, ELIS, *Neath and district*, 1974.

JOHN, W. D., *English Lustre Pottery*, 1962.

JONES, I., *Printing and Printers in Wales and Monmouthshire*, 1925.

JONES, W. H., *History of the Port of Swansea*, 1922.

JONES, W. H., *History of Swansea*, 1920.

LLOYD, THOMAS, *The Lost Houses of Wales*, 1986.

MATTHEWS, Directory of Swansea, 1816 and 1830.

MORGAN, T. J., 'Place Names' in *Swansea and its Regions*, Ed. W. G. V. Balchen, 1971.

NANCE, MORTON, *The Pottery and Porcelain of Swansea and Nantgarw*, 1942.

OWEN, BRYN, *History of the Welsh Militia and Voluntary Corps, 1757-1968, Vol. 3*, 1994.

PHILLIPS, RHYS, *The History of The Vale of Neath*, 1925.

POLLINS, H., 'The Swansea Canal' in *The Journal of Transport History*, 1954.

P. R. Office Rail Papers 87/12/3.

PRYCE, P. & WILLIAMS, S., *Swansea Blue and White Pottery*, 1972.

REES, R. D., *South Wales and Monmouthshire Newspapers under the Stamp Acts*, 1962.

RILEY, N., *Gifts for Good Children*, 1991.

ROBERTS, R. O., 'Financial crisis and the Swansea Branch Bank of England, 1826' in *The National Library of Wales Journal XI*, 1958.

ROGERS, W. C., *The Swansea and Glamorgan Calendar Pt 2* (Manuscript, unpublished).

SHAW, SIMEON, *The Rise and Fall of the Staffordshire Potteries*, 1829.

TEULON-PORTER, N., *The Teulon Porter Collection of Mocha Pottery*, Museum and Art Gallery, Stoke on Trent, 1953.

WHITER, L., *Spode*, 1970.

WILLIAMS, S. H., 'Sherds from the Cambrian and Glamorgan Potteries' published in *Mediaeval and later Pottery in Wales*, 9, 1986-87.

Appendix I

AGREEMENT FORMS BETWEEN CO-PARTNERS AND WORKMEN, dated 1837

Reproduced by permission of Swansea Museum, Swansea City Council.

Appendix II

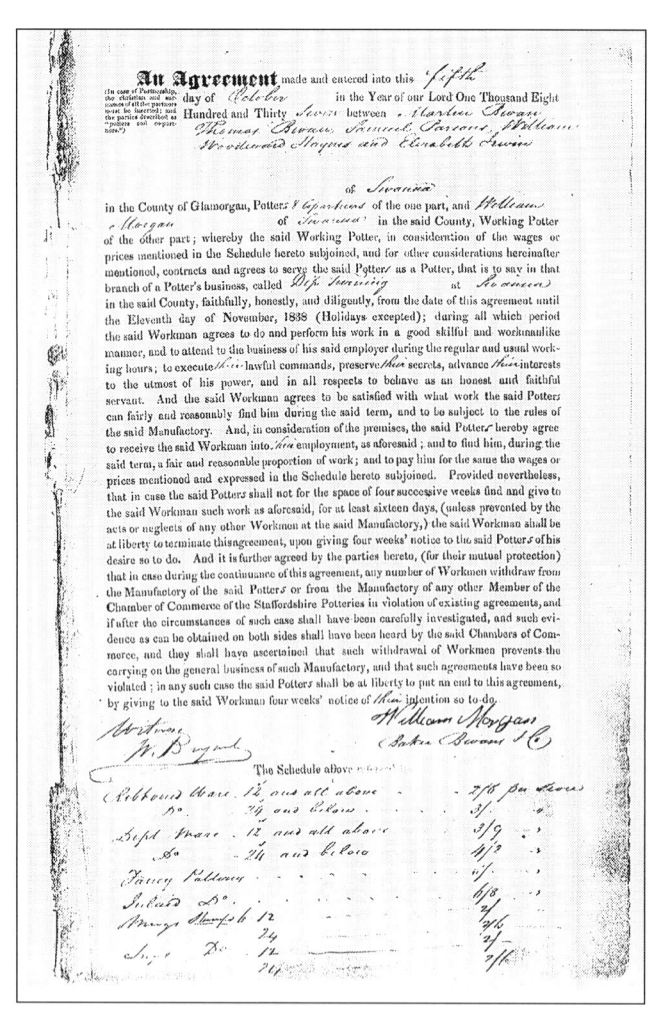

WILLIAM BRYANT'S WORKBOOK
Watermarked 'Hall 1831'

Reproduced by kind permission of South Glamorgan County Library, Cardiff. (Ref. Cardiff Ms. 2.9444)

Transcript of hand-written recipes

Glamorgan Pottery Glazes etc.

Orange Under Glaze
6th Red Lead
1¼th Crocus Martis
5th Glos of Antimony
¾th Flint. All these must be well mixed and to be fired at the bottom of the [fore being] in Biscuit Kiln.

To prepare Tin Ashes for Yellow
Take 120 of lead and 30 of Tin burnt in usual manner
6th of the above Tin Ashes
1½ of Crude Antimony
1½ Litharge to be fired at the bottom of the [fore being] of the Biscuit Kiln.

To prepare Blue for Comn. Green Colour
16 oz Best Calx
14 oz Flint
14 oz Glos
 3 oz China Clay
24 oz Litharge
 8 oz Nitre to be fired in 4 in the Glos Kiln. Four times the above quantity will fill a plat. Saggar.

Common Green
6 oz of the above Blue
7½ oz Biscuit Yellow ground well together

20 Make Matt Blue
6th Murur of Alum
1 Oxide of Zinc
¾ Flint Glos
½ Ground Blue
The above mixed and fired on top of Biscuit Kiln, then ground for use.

French Green
3½th Flint
1½ of Borax
1½ oxide of Tin
6 oz Green chrome
6 oz Ground Blue
The above mixed and fired on top of Biscuit Kiln, then ground for use.

Victoria Green
3th Flint
3th Whiting
2th Dichromate of Potash
2th Sugar of lead
1th Borax
3th Chromate of Lead
} This mixed and fired at top of Biscuit Kiln twice, then ground for use.

Torque Stain
4th of Oxide of Zinc
3th Barytes
1th Blue
Mix the above, fired it on top of Glos Kiln, then ground for use—3ths will stain 40 gallons of slip.

Best Glaze I made at Llanelly
22 China Clay
48 Stone
18 Flint
18 Carbonate of Lime
10 Borax
The glaze is made as follows.
To every 120th of the above fritt, add 20th of White Lead and 3oz Blue Calc. for stain.

Chrome Green from Dr Ure's Book
1th of Chromate of Potash
½th flowers of Sulphur dissolved in boiling water till the green oxide precipitates. The above compound may be made in a crucible by calcining and washed clean.

Red from Chromate of Potash
Nitre brought to fusion in a crucible at a gentle heat, pure chrome yellow is to be thrown in by a small portion at a time—the yellow is to be thrown in till a little of the nitre remains, must not overheat the crucible or the colour will come brown, after settled a little time, then pour off the top and the Red powder will be at the bottom of the crucible.

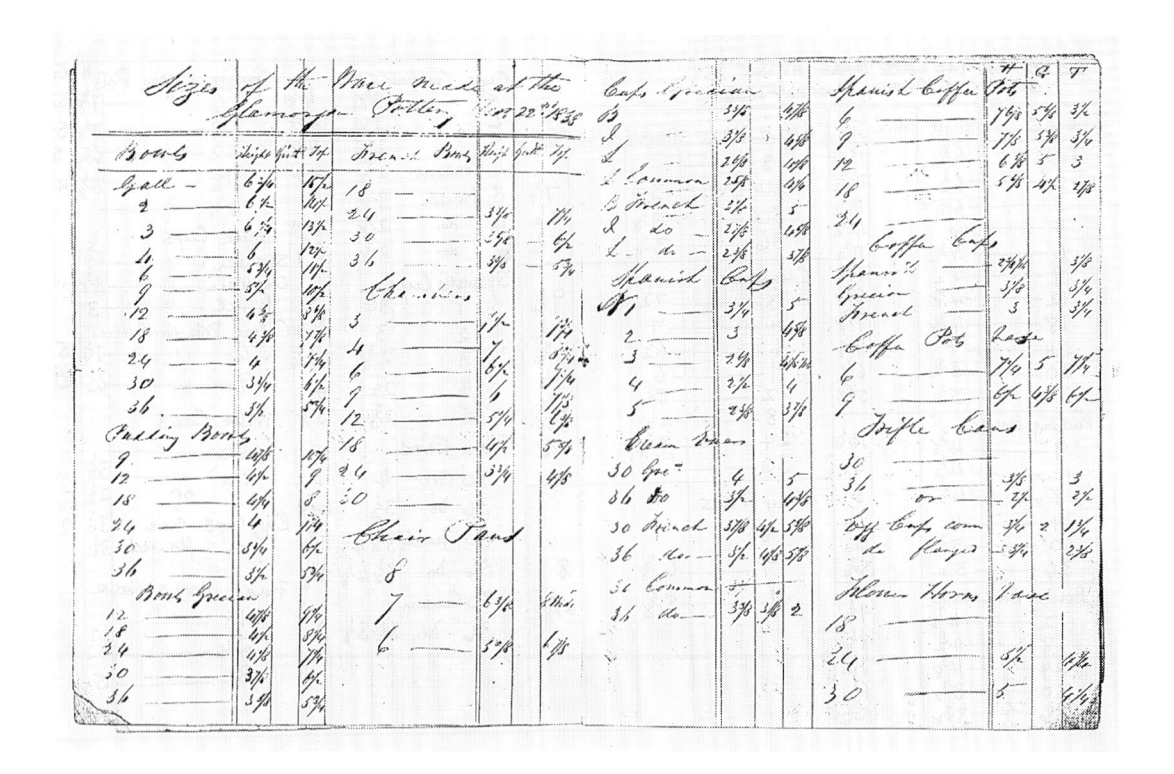

Transcript

SIZES OF THE WARE MADE AT THE GLAMORGAN POTTERY NOV 22nd 1838									H.	G.	T.		H.	G.	T.
BOWLS	Height	Girth	Top	French Bowls	Height	Girth	Top	Cups Grecian				Spanish Coffee Pots			
Gall.	6¾		15½	18				B	3⅜		4⅞	6	7⅞	5⅝	3½
2	6½		14½	24	3⅞		7¼	L	3⅛		4⅝	9	7⅛	5⅜	3¼
3	6¼		13½	30	3⅝		6½	S	2⅞		4⅛	12	6⅝	5	3
4	6		12½	36	3⅝		5¾	L Common	2⅝		4¼	18	5⅝	4½	2⅞
6	5¾		11½					B French	3⅛		5	24			
9	5½		10½					L do.	2⅞		4⅝				
12	4⅞		8⅞	Chambers				S do.	2⅜		3⅞	Coffee Cups			
18	4⅜		7⅞	3	7½		9¾					Spanish	2⅝		3⅛
24	4		4¼	4	7		8¾	Spanish Cups				Grecian	3⅛		3¼
30	3¾		6½	6	6½		7¾	1	3¼		5	French	3		3¼
36	3½		5⅝	9	6		7⅛	2	3		4⅝	Coffee Pots			
				12	5¼		6⅜	3	2⅞		4¼ 1/16	6	7¼	5	7¼
Pudding Bowls				18	4½		5⅝	4	2½		4	9	6½	4⅝	6½
9	4⅞		10¼	24	3¾		4⅛	5	2⅝		3⅞				
12	4½		9	30								Trifle Cans			
18	4½		8									30			
24	4		7¼	Chair Pans				Cream Ewers				36	3⅛		3
30	3¾		6½	8				30 Gre.	4		5	or	2½		2½
36	3½		5¾	7	6⅜		8	36 Do.	3½		4⅜	Egg cups comm.	3¼	2	1⅜
				6	5⅞		6⅞	30 French	3⅞	4½	5⅝	do. flanged	3¼		2¾
Bowls Grecian								36 Do.	3½	4⅛	5⅛				
12	4⅞		9¼					30 Common				Flower Horns Vase			
18	4½		8¼					36 Do.	3⅜	3⅛	2	18			
24	4⅛		7¼									24	5½		4¾
30	3⅞		6½									30	5		4¼
36	3⅝		5¾												

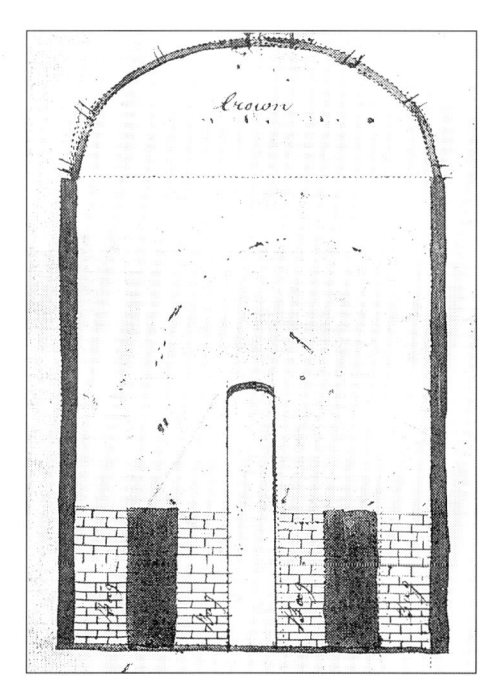

Among the most fascinating details to be found in William Bryant's workbook are the notes and diagrams giving specifications of kilns.

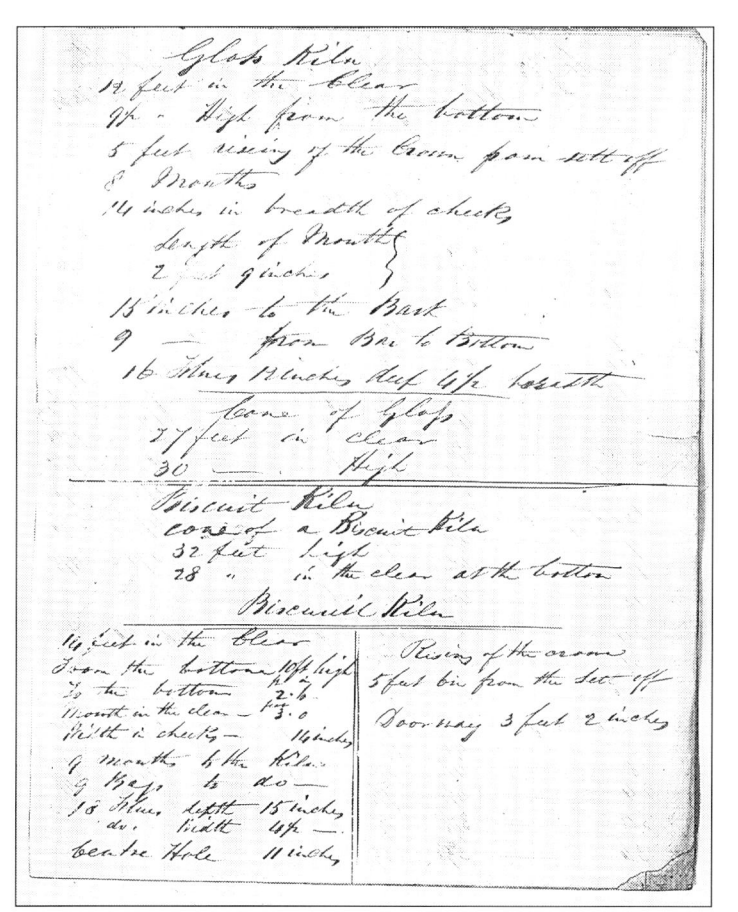

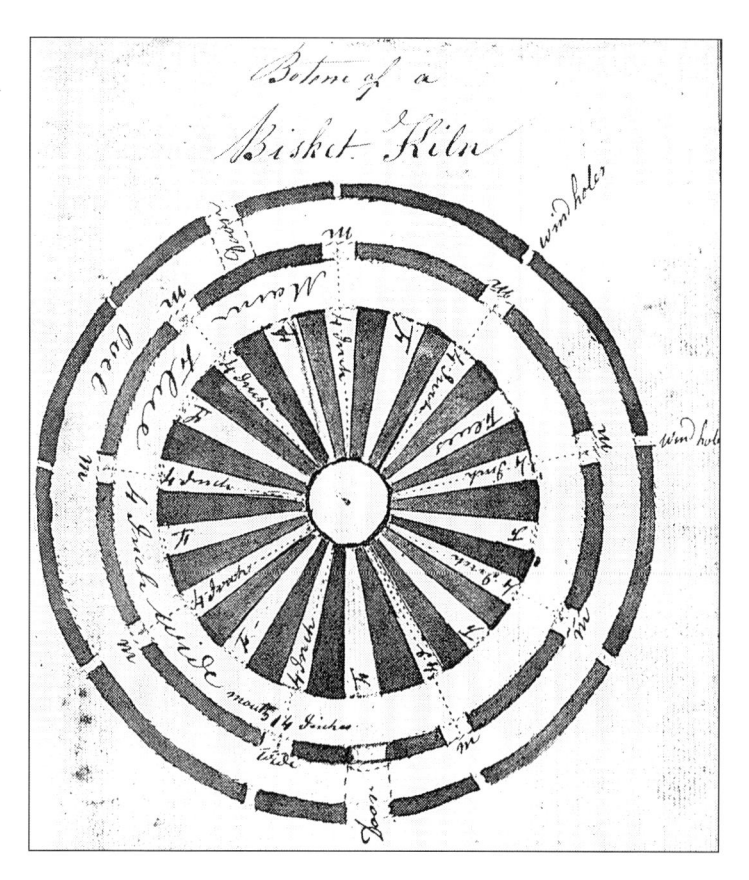

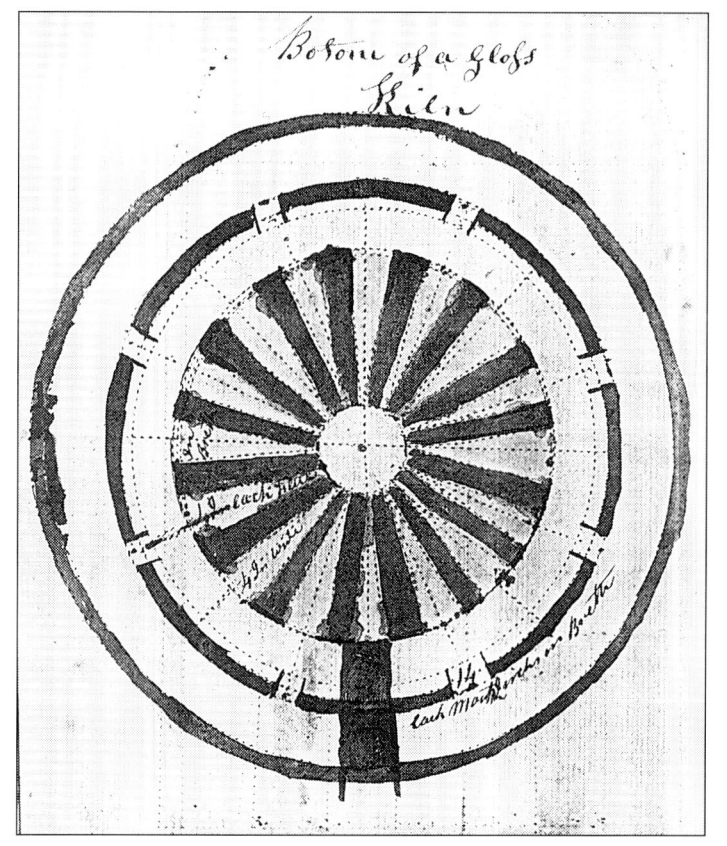

Index to Illustrations of Wares

Arcaded plates Pl. 3; 111.
Banded ware Pl. 102.
Coffee pots Pl .123-126.
Cow creamers Pl. 160-162.
Creamware Pl. 1; 2.
Cream jugs Pl. 34; 68; 139-144.
Cups/saucers Pl. 9; 60; 82; 84-85; 145-149.
Dessert dish Pl. 113.
Egg cup stand Pl. 152.
Feather-edged plates Pl. 7; 8.
Filled in transfers Pl. 9-31; 122; 128; 138-142.
Footbath Pl. 155/6.
Gravy boat Pl. 108.
Green glazed wares Pl. 95-98.
Hand painted wares Pl. 4-8; 44.
Jugs, Glamorgan shape Pl. 4-6; 44-46; 48/9; 52; 67; 72-81; 117-119.
Jugs, other shapes Pl. 35; 37; 39-43; 50; 112.
Marbled ware Pl. 102.
Marks Pl. 93/4; 167-179.
Meat platters Pl. 103/4.
Miniature plates Pl. 10; 12-31; 36; 63-66; 110; 166.
Mugs Pl. 70/1; 150/1.
Mustard pot Pl. 112.
Mocha ware Pl. 102.
Patterns
   Birds & Flowers Pl. 32.
   Bridge & Tower Pl. 33; 34; 150.
   Broseley Pl. 35; 36; 151; 152; 159.
   Campania Pl. 37; 136; 141; 148.
   Castle Gatehouse Pl. 38; 103; 113; 114; 155/6.
   Commemorative Wares:
      O'Connell Jug Pl. 42; 43.
      Reform Jugs Pl. 39; 40; 41.
   Continuous Sheet Patterns:
      Bells Pl. 47.
      Quilted Pl. 48.
      'Vine' Pl. 49; 140; 149.
   'Cottage Girl' Pl. 50; 126; 129.
   Cowherd Pl. 51; 130.
   Floral Pl. 52; 104; 105; 106; 111.
   'Gothic Border' Pl. 53; 54.
   'Harper' Pl. 55; 127.
   'Haymaker' Pl. 56; 131.
   Ladies of Llangollen Pl. 57; 115; 116.
   Mandarin & Lantern Pl. 58; 132.
   Mandarin & Pipe Pl. 59; 124; 146.
   Parrot Pl. 60.
   Pulteney Bridge Bath Pl. 61; 62; 121; 154; 163/4.
   Rural Pl. 63-81; 117-119; 134/5; 137; 143-145; 160; 166.
   Shells & Flowers Pl. 82; 110; 112; 133; 147; 165.
   Shepherd Pl. 83; 84; 85; 125.
   Ships Pl. 86-89.
   Stylised Floral Pl. 90; 108; 109; 123; 139.
   Tower Pl. 91; 120; 153; 155/6; 157/8.
   Willow Pl. 92; 93; 94; 107.
Personal commemoratives Pl. 4; 44; 45/6.
Pickle dish Pl. 114.
Pierced basket Pl. 115/6.
Plates Pl. 57-59; 86-90; 92-94.
Puzzle jug Pl. 163/4.
Salad bowl Pl. 105.
Shards Pl. 102.
Slop bowls Pl. 53-56; 83; 138.
Sprigged jugs Pl. 99-101.
Strainer Pl. 109.
Sugar bowls Pl. 136/7.
Teapots Pl. 11; 32/3; 47; 51; 69; 129-135.
Toilet Wares Pl. 153-159.
Toothbrush boxes Pl. 153; 159.
Tureen/bases Pl. 38; 106.
Vase Pl. 165.
Vegetable dishes Pl. 107.
Water jugs/bowls Pl. 61/2; 91; 120/1; 154; 157/8.